The Christian Cosmic Narrative
The Deep History of the World

Foreword by Fr. John Riccardo

The Christian Cosmic Narrative
The Deep History of the World

Layout and Cover Design by Jacqueline L. Challiss Hill

Cover image by Tetra Images, Turkey, Istanbul,
Mosaic of Christ Pantocrator in Hagia Sophia Mosque.

ISBN: 978-1-7364920-0-0

Library of Congress Control Number: 2021932562

Printed in the United States

XXIX
PRESS

Published by ACTS XXIX Press
1050 Porter St.
Detroit, MI 48226
actsxxix.org | press@actsxxix.org

"C. S. Lewis wrote that reason is the organ of truth but imagination is the organ of meaning. Something may be true but it lacks any meaning if our imagination doesn't 'get it.' When Israel strayed from keeping the commandments, Moses insisted on retelling the story of their exodus from Egypt. He needed to stir their imagination and reawaken their sense of gratitude and vocation. If we want to keep the commandments, we must recover the story behind them. Story enlivens our imagination and sense of moral purpose. Knowing our story establishes our identity, and, in this age of identity politics, we need to enter into that story or be at the mercy of scores of distorted stories about the history and shape of the world.

"*The Christian Cosmic Narrative* lays out the 'deep history of our world' and our place in the grand scheme of things. It lifts the curtain on the invisible conflicts that permeate our visible world. This is a drama that boils over with emotional intensity and moral seriousness as we follow the decisions of unusual, often iconic, characters. Decisions have consequences. The plot is filled with twists, betrayals, and rebellions. We see the mighty fall and the lowly lifted up. At other times, we find ourselves in the grip of ecstatic visions of future glory and triumphal moments of liberation. It is the history of the world in which God is the storyteller and chief protagonist. It is our adventure of discipleship.

"In *The Christian Cosmic Narrative*, we see God's purposes unfolding through the world he created, the creatures he called, and the futures that humans will decide to inhabit. This is the story of your life. Read it and rejoice, or read it and weep."

Al Kresta
President and CEO of Ave Maria Radio
and Host of "Kresta in the Afternoon"

"One of the greatest challenges the Church is currently facing is rediscovering and communicating what many of us have lost: The Great Story. The result has been that most people live in a world without God. In this post-modern world, where reality is either reduced to the level of the material or is believed to be capable of being endlessly manipulated, Christians need to be told The Story that reveals the truth about the world in which we live. This book captures and re-tells in a captivating way the earth-shattering truths of this world *with* God...and what a life with God might look like."

Father Mike Schmitz
Director, Diocese of Duluth Office of Youth Ministry
Chaplain, University of Minnesota-Duluth Newman
Catholic Campus Ministries

"To be captured by the Good News of the Gospel is to encounter the grand, epic adventure of life with God. *The Christian Cosmic Narrative* cuts through all the boredom of repetition and familiarity and presents the Faith for what it truly is: the greatest story ever told, the very story in which we live."

Msgr. James P. Shea
President, University of Mary

"People are drawn to story, whether it be found in a movie, book, or a grandfather recalling the past. Today, at this moment in time, your life has been influenced by where you think we came from and where you think we are headed. If we don't understand the true overarching story of the universe, we may find ourselves living in a tiny, incomplete, and counterfeit subplot of God's cosmic narrative. Every Christian is obligated to understand and faithfully respond to God's revelation, and all Christians must become storytellers."

Jeff Cavins
Founder and Creator of *The Great Adventure Bible Study*

"I had always believed that the world involved magic: now I thought that perhaps it involved a magician. And this pointed to a profound emotion always present and sub-conscious; that this world of ours has some purpose; and if there is a purpose, there is a person. I had always felt life first as a story: and if there is a story there is a story-teller. . . .

"This is the thrilling romance of Orthodoxy. People have fallen into a foolish habit of speaking of orthodoxy as something heavy, humdrum, and safe. There never was anything so perilous or so exciting as orthodoxy. It was sanity: and to be sane is more dramatic than to be mad. It was the equilibrium of a man behind madly rushing horses, seeming to stoop this way and to sway that, yet in every attitude having the grace of statuary and the accuracy of arithmetic. . . .and in my vision the heavenly chariot flies thundering through the ages, the dull heresies sprawling and prostrate, the wild truth reeling but erect."

~ G. K. Chesterton, *Heretics and Orthodoxy*

"Let us recall the myths of countless peoples in which heroes pleasing to the divinity were lifted, and taking their destiny with them, were fixed in some constellations. Thus man and his fate, that so vulnerable and yet so significant scrap of life and eventfulness, is exalted to an eternal image beyond the reach of all history, itself now an eternal shaper of history. . . .What does this signify? That Jesus Christ, who was born in Nazareth, lived in Palestine; who taught, suffered, died and rose again, blazes above the world an eternally valid 'constellation' that lights and directs all creation; that he is 'sign,' prototype, meaning, measure and order of all that is. The Redeemer's existence. . . .is not limited by geographical or racial boundaries, but enfolds the universe."

~ Romano Guardini, *The Lord*

"The Gospels contain a fairy-story, or a story of a larger kind which embraces all the essence of fairy-stories. They contain many marvels—peculiarly artistic, beautiful, and moving: 'mythical' in their perfect, self-contained significance; and among the marvels is the greatest and most complete conceivable eucatastrophe. But this story has entered History and the primary world; the desire and aspiration of sub-creation has been raised to the fulfillment of Creation. The Birth of Christ is the eucatastrophe of Man's history. The Resurrection is the eucatastrophe of the story of the Incarnation. This story begins and ends in joy. It has pre-eminently the 'inner consistency of reality.' There is no tale ever told that men would rather find was true, and none which so many skeptical men have accepted as true on its own merits. For the Art of it has the supremely convincing tone of Primary Art, that is, of Creation. To reject it leads either to sadness or to wrath."

~ J. R. R. Tolkien, *Tolkien On Fairy-stories*

"Jesus is no myth. He is a man of flesh and blood and he stands as a fully real part of history. We can go to the very places where he himself went. We can hear his words through his witnesses. He died and he is risen. It is as if the mysterious Passion contained in bread had waited for him, had stretched out its arms toward him; it is as if the myths had waited for him, because in him what they long for came to pass."

~ Pope Benedict XVI, *Jesus of Nazareth:*
From the Baptism in the Jordan to the Transfiguration

"The heart of Christianity is a myth which is also a fact. . . .By becoming a fact, it does not cease to be a myth. That is the miracle. . . .Christians need to be reminded that what became fact was a myth; that it carries with it into the world of fact all the properties of a myth. . . .We must not be ashamed of the mythical radiance resting on our theology.

"For this is the marriage of heaven and earth: perfect myth and perfect fact, claiming not only our love and our obedience but also our wonder and delight, addressed to the savage, the child, and the poet in each one of us no less than the moralist, the scholar, and the philosopher.

"It is the myth that gives life."

~ C. S. Lewis, *God in the Dock*

"In the final analysis, specialized theological knowledge can take us only so far; we need to know the *story*."

~ Fleming Rutledge, *The Crucifixion:*
Understanding the Death of Jesus Christ

Table of Contents

PART III:

SHADOW TO REALITY: THE COMING OF THE MESSIAH

PART IV:

THE LAST DAYS: THE MESSIANIC AGE

Foreword

This is a book about hope.

"Always be prepared to make a defense to any one who calls you to account for the hope that is in you" (1 Pet. 3:15). So wrote St. Peter, a personal friend of Jesus, to some of the first Christians in the middle of the first century.

Ours is an age desperate for reasons to hope. 2018 was the first time in nearly one hundred years that life expectancy in the United States declined for a third consecutive year. The last time that happened the world was just coming out of World War I and entering the Spanish flu. Now, however, sociologists tell us that we are living shorter and dying sooner because of what they call "deaths of despair." Enormous numbers of people, of all ages and ethnicities, all races, all socioeconomic spheres, are losing the will to live. There are many reasons for this, to be sure, but I would argue the ultimate reason is because people have no hope.

That's where this book comes in, and why I believe it is so urgent. The first Christians knew they had reasons—concrete, historical, true reasons for hope. They knew that faith is not blind, but in fact enables us to see. They knew that faith isn't squishy, it isn't contrary to reason, it isn't some made-up story. The first Christians knew that faith is the greatest of all stories and that we are living smack in the middle of the greatest story ever told.

The Christian faith is the true story that makes known to us why anything exists at all. It's the story of how God, "the only really interesting personality in existence," Creator of all things, visible and invisible, not only made everything that is but of how he made us in his own image and likeness not to be his slaves but to be his friends and to share in his own divine and abundant life for all eternity.

The Christian faith is the true story that makes known to us how everything went wrong, how it all got so messed up. We could call this "the bad news," if you will. Faith enables us to know that one of God's good creatures rebelled against him and went to war against us, the creature God loves most of all. Faith enables us to see that this creature, far more powerful than we can imagine, captured us at the dawn of our race, deceiving us to join in his rebellion so that he could enslave us to powers against which we cannot compete, most especially the power of Death.

The Christian faith is the true story that makes known to us that God did not sit idly by and let us stay captured, but rather acted in an extraordinary, unexpected, and shocking way: he became one of us, a man, so as to do battle against our ancient enemy and to rescue us from his grip and the power of Death, making it possible for us once again to share in the destiny for which God created us.

The Christian faith is the true story that makes known to us that the truly great adventure in life is to respond with all of our heart, mind, soul, and strength to what God has done for us in Jesus.

Peter knew all of this, and that was why he had hope. The first Christians, too, knew this, and in the midst of a Roman Empire that was riddled with anxiety and despair they shone forth like bright and shining lamps because of their hope.

In many ways, ours is an age like that of the first Christians. To be sure, we have many conveniences and entertainments that far exceed theirs, and we have advanced in science and medicine and other fields beyond what they could have imagined. But like those first Christians, we are surrounded by people who have never heard the story, never heard the gospel, and who are riddled with anxiety, fear, and despair.

In fact, many Church-going Christians have never heard the gospel, at least not in a compelling and life-changing way. And, until we do, nothing will really ever make any sense. We won't understand why we're here, where we're going, or how to get there.

Pope John Paul II once wrote that hearing the ardent proclamation of the gospel, of the extraordinary and unexpected news of what God has done for the world in Jesus, should result in a person being overwhelmed and brought to a decision to surrender himself to Jesus in faith. That's what happened to the early Christians who met the first friends of Jesus and who heard their proclamation of his life, death, and resurrection from the dead. The result of their hearing the gospel was that over a remarkably short period of time Christianity in the Roman Empire went from being an illegal superstition that was not infrequently persecuted to becoming the official religion of that same Empire.

At the heart of the gospel is this proclamation: You matter! You are loved far, far, far more than you ever could have imagined. You are worth the trouble! You are worth the trouble of God creating you, of his becoming man to rescue you from powers worse than your worst nightmare, of his desire for you to be an active agent in the work of re-creation that he began on Easter Sunday, and of his calling you to abundant and unending life where there is no pain, sorrow, or death.

The pages that follow break open this story in a truly remarkable way, and we are delighted to share it with you. It is our prayer that this book will help remedy the anxiety and hopelessness that is so prevalent all around us and perhaps in our own lives. May our hearts be overwhelmed, either for the first time or anew, as we turn the page and truly enter into the greatest story ever told.

~ Fr. John Riccardo
   Executive Director, ACTS XXIX

Prime Matters

An audio version of the narrative in this book is
available at no cost from
Prime Matters: primematters.com/narrative.
Prime Matters, a project of
educational outreach of the University of Mary,
exists to awaken the Catholic imaginative vision
in Catholics and all people of goodwill.

Prologue

Humans are inveterate meaning-seeking beings, and because of that we are indefatigable myth-makers: we gain meaning for our lives by understanding the story we are in and the part we are playing in that story. We refer to that narrative in order to assess our progress and to understand our identity. We cannot function without such a cosmic story. In putting together this account of the Christian cosmic narrative, we are assuming that "myth" in this sense does not mean "*false* story." We hold instead that "myth" means "*meaningful* story," an overall narrative that allows us to make sense of our existence. A given mythic narrative, like a particular religion, may be true or false, or likely—as in most religions—a mixture of truth and falsehood; but those who hold to a myth, like those who believe a religion, always think it expresses important truths. We want to make the claim that every individual, and every collective group of humans, necessarily goes forward in life under the influence of some kind of cosmic mythic story. Our mythic picture of the world is our understanding of the narrative we are living and the meaning of that narrative for our day-to-day existence and for our ultimate destiny.

If our cosmic vision of the world goes into serious crisis, so do we; and if we cannot resolve the crisis, we either end our lives or stupefy ourselves with addictive distractions. Even those who say they have abandoned all narratives and have left behind all meta-stories have not really done so; they have only constructed stories of negation and revolt. There is simply no doing away with such narratives of meaning. Given this, it is perhaps not surprising that God's revelation to the human race comes largely in the form of a story, a "salvation history." Humans have always loved stories. Epic narratives have dominated our imagination, from the Homeric poems and the Icelandic Eddas to more recent examples like Tolkien's *Lord of the Rings*, the Star Wars saga, the Harry Potter series, and the constant stream of Marvel superhero tales. We are drawn to drama because we are made for stories; because we are living in the midst of a story; because we know that everything for us depends—individually and for our race as a whole—on the outcome of the story in which we find ourselves.

Much of what it means to be converted in mind to Christianity is to understand and embrace the Christian narrative, the true cosmic story within which each individual life can find meaning and direction. Our current age has devised myths of its own, narratives of meaning that have become so prevalent that they are assumed by most of us as self-evident. The modern progressive narrative inhabits our atmosphere, and we take it in through our pores. Part of the challenge for modern Christians is that we are attempting to live the Christian life amid a culture that has abandoned the Christian story and has replaced it with a different cosmic narrative, one that is intrinsically hostile to Christianity. Many who call themselves Christians have consciously, if incoherently, adopted the modern progressive myth even as they continue to use categories and language that come from Christianity. Many others who are believing Christians have been deeply affected by the modern cosmic story without fully realizing how much it has shaped their identity and their understanding of the world. The goal of this work is to present an account of the Christian narrative in its broad outlines and its dramatic sweep, such that it can be embraced (or rejected) authentically.

It is good to remember that Christianity is a historical religion. This means more than the fact that Christianity arose at a given time among a particular group of people, or that it has left its mark in the historical record. The same could be said of all religions. To say that Christianity is historical means that the Christian religion, like the Jewish faith out of which it sprung and upon which it depends, is necessarily founded on specific historical events. Christianity is not an escape from time; it is rather a redemption through time and history.

We can see the significance of this historical quality if we compare Christianity with other significant religious traditions and pose certain historical questions to them. If it could be shown beyond reasonable doubt that the figure of Buddha was legendary and never really existed, what would happen to Buddhism? Probably not much; the Buddhist religion would not be significantly affected. Buddha introduced a path of spiritual wisdom to his followers. Whatever his qualities as a person, the path itself is the essential element and would remain intact even if its origins were unclear. What is true of Buddhism is yet more decisively true of Hinduism: there is no great founder of the Hindu religion upon whose actions its beliefs rest. The same quality marks all the great religious philosophies. Confucius, Plato, Lao Tzu, and Zeno were remarkable people and we are interested in whatever we can find out about them, about what they said and how they lived. Still, the philosophies they put forward would lose nothing of their grandeur and wisdom even if little were known of their founders. But what happens when we ask the same question of Christianity? What if it were proven that Jesus of Nazareth had never lived, or had never risen from the dead? Such a discovery would destroy the Christian faith. *If Christ has not been raised,* wrote St. Paul to the Corinthians, *then our preaching is in vain and your faith is in vain* (1 Cor. 15:14). The strength (or weakness) of the Christian claim depends on the reliability of its history.

This historical aspect of Christianity is important because it has momentous consequences concerning the Christian account of reality. Christianity is not fundamentally a philosophy, though Christians have developed impressive philosophic systems. It is not mainly a code of ethics, though the Christian faith clarifies the moral order and makes serious moral demands on its followers. It is not primarily a practical plan for the betterment of the existing world, though Christians have had much to say about that. At its heart, Christianity is an epic adventure, a high romance, one whose hero and primary actor is God, and one that has implications of infinite importance for every person living. As C. S. Lewis put it in *God in the Dock*, "The heart of Christianity is a myth which is also a fact." It is historical and it is mythical at the same time.

Our plan is to recount the Christian narrative, to sketch the outline of this gripping story. It has all the hallmarks of an epic saga. It deals with love and sacrifice. It includes danger in dark places and courage against all odds. There is beauty and terror, hope and despair, glorious battle and malicious betrayal. It contains humor and irony, depth of character, folly, and profound insight. It confronts us with the gloomy chasm of death, and it opens us upon a dawn of bursting life. And this intriguing tale is yet more wonderful because it happens to be true. It is the story behind every story, the tale from which every tale rises. It is the true adventure of the human race, and the underlying drama of every individual life.

The sacred Scriptures are the primary source for our understanding of the Christian narrative. The Scriptures, written under the inspiration of the Holy Spirit by the Old and New Testament Church, and interpreted with ever deepening understanding by the Church through the years, is the narrative's irreplaceable foundation. Beyond the Scriptures, certain interpretive voices from the tradition have been tapped for the construction of this account as characteristic of the way the story has been told through the years: among others, Irenaeus of Lyon, Athanasius of Alexandria, Gregory of Nyssa, Augustine of Hippo, John Damascene, Thomas Aquinas, Blaise Pascal, John Henry Newman, G. K. Chesterton, J. R. R. Tolkien, and Joseph Ratzinger.

The narrative given here follows the Scriptures and the Great Tradition, and so in its broad lines repeats the story Christians have received and handed on from the beginning. But the specifics of how this magnificent tale is told, in tone, emphasis, and completeness, can differ for many reasons. John the Evangelist wrote that all the books in the world could not contain what Jesus said and did; and since his time the world has been filled with books examining every aspect of the Christian narrative from every possible point of view. The account given here is meant as a guideline, necessarily imperfect and claiming no originality, and those using it should be free to amend, amplify, or improve it as they see fit, provided they also use the sources of revelation and the Great Tradition as their basis.

Christianity is the most thrilling story ever seriously believed by large numbers of people over long periods of time. We may run into someone who says: "I see what Christians think, hope, and believe; I feel the power of the Christian narrative; I understand its attraction; I can see why so many people through the ages have risked everything for it and based the whole of their lives on it. But I haven't embraced it because I haven't found my way to believing that the story the Christians tell is true." In such a case, we know we are dealing with a sensible, if mistaken, person holding a reasonable position. But if we meet someone who says, "The problem with Christianity is that it is colorless, boring, humdrum, and conventional; I'm looking for something more interesting, more elevating, more inspiring, something richer and more gripping," then we know that we're dealing with someone who is ignorant of Christianity and who has never heard its account of reality. Sadly, many Christians are themselves in this ignorant state. So, an important task for all Christians is to understand the Christian story: to see the broad lines of the great drama into which we have been born, and in which we have been assigned a momentous part to play.

PART I
GOD, CREATION, AND FALL

Chapter 1
God

Our story begins, as all true stories must begin, with that mighty and mysterious being beyond all imagining and above all that is, the source and center of existence: God. God, the infinite in being; God, the essence of goodness; God, the fountain of life; God, the all-powerful and all-knowing; God, the wellspring of truth; God, the "alpha and omega," the beginning and the end of all meaning; God, the beautiful, the aching if often unnamed desire of every human heart.

What can we say about this mysterious Being who plays the central role in the human drama? Here is how the Great Tradition speaks of him: "Uncreated, without beginning, immortal, infinite, eternal, immaterial, good, creative, just, enlightening, immutable, passionless, uncircumscribed, immeasurable, unlimited, undefined, unseen, unthinkable, wanting in nothing, being his own rule and authority, all-ruling, life-giving, omnipotent, of infinite power, containing and maintaining the universe and making provision for all: possessing all these and such like attributes by nature, not having received them from elsewhere, but himself imparting all good to his own creations according to the capacity of each."[1]

---

1 *St. John of Damascus: Writings: The Fount of Knowledge; The Philosophical Chapters; On Heresies; The Orthodox Faith [The Fathers of the Church, Vol. 3]. (*Online: Ex Fontibus Co., 2015), 176.

God has revealed his name as "The One Who Is" (cf. Exod. 3:14). God is the one Being who can be said simply to exist. Anything else that might exist exists at a different and lower plane, and exists only by participating in the existence of the One who Is. God exists outside of time and place. He is not the greatest of the various things that exist, as one among many lesser beings. He is not the most powerful "thing" in the universe. He is not a "thing" at all. He is beyond all that he has created; he is utterly distinct from all that he has brought into being, and yet at the same time he is the very ground of its existence. He transcends any possible category or description we may have of him. He Is.

This incomprehensible being has revealed himself as both one as unchangeable, simple in perfection, unable to be divided, and three—Father, Son, and Spirit—each personal and yet beyond our experience of what it means to be personal.

Among the many titles of God, the one that perhaps touches his inner being most closely is the one that tells us that God *is* love. By this is meant that in the very structure of his being God instantiates all that is meant by love. The Father utters himself, pours himself out, empties himself entirely by an act of self-gift, begetting from all eternity the Son, speaking from all eternity his Word, the *Logos*. The Son, with an equal act of loving self-gift, empties himself completely in giving place to and returning the whole of himself to the Father. The perfection of their offering of self, one to the other, brings forth from all eternity the Spirit, who then pours himself out completely and perfectly on behalf of Father and Son. Trinity in Unity: love in perfect action, a fountain of life and mutual gift springing up at the center of all that is, a dance of harmonious music enjoying in timeless perfection the essence of goodness, life, love, beauty, and truth. God: the only really interesting personality in existence.

For reasons that are ultimately beyond our comprehension, but that have to do with his loving desire to share his life and his goodness,

God determined to create, to bring into existence realities other than himself. When God performed his creative act, the Father brought forth all of creation through the Son, his "Word." Everything that existed came into being through and for the Son. God first brought about the invisible, spiritual world, and then he created the visible, material world. The spiritual realm of his creation was to be higher, richer, vaster, and more beautiful than the material realm. But the material world was to have a beauty and a purpose of its own in expressing the infinite creativity of the Divine mind. This decision on God's part to create marks the beginning of our drama, the adventure of the human race.

Chapter 2
Spiritual Creation
and the Fall of Lucifer

When God decided to create, to bring into existence a world outside of himself yet intrinsically related to him by its participation in his existence, he began by calling forth the first creatures of his thought, the noblest of all created beings: the angels. Resembling God by the gift of intelligent minds and free wills, angels were meant to live in the joy of God's presence, delighting in him, serving him, and joining in his eternal dance of love. They were to be his special aides, his messengers and stewards, and were to have an important role in governing and caring for the second part of creation yet to come, that of the material world.

Many different kinds and ranks of angels were created, each with special qualities of excellence, each participating in and reflecting an aspect of the infinite Divine mind that had brought them into being. Their numbers were vast beyond counting, and their light and power as they basked in and reflected the potent loving gaze of their Creator were a marvel of beauty beyond description. Noteworthy among them was the mighty archangel Michael, whose name was a tribute to the greatness of God.

Among the myriads of angels, the creature in whom God infused the greatest portion of his power and his gifts was given the name Lucifer, the "light bearer," the "daystar." He was highly favored by his Maker, meant to occupy a unique place in God's creative plan and to reflect God's goodness with an unequaled splendor.

Like all the angelic beings, Lucifer had been graced with the gift of free will, a gift that allowed the exercise of genuine love. But the gift of freedom and the door it opened upon a glorious destiny came also with a perilous possibility: that the one who was free to love was also free to turn away from love in self-centered pride. Lucifer thus faced a necessary choice: either to embrace his created being and participate in the life and love of the God who had made him and upon whom his existence depended, or to foolishly declare his independence from his Maker and, by falling into delusion, insist on calling himself the source of his own life.

Lucifer chose the blindness of pride. He became enamored of his own beauty and strength, and set himself to be independent of his Maker. Our biblical sources tell us that he fell from his high place out of envy. His envy was most significantly directed at God. He wanted not to serve, but to rule. He resented the fact of his created and derivative nature. He also envied a not-yet-created humanity. He perceived that in fulfilling the role God had planned for him, according to heaven's logic of love he would be called upon to serve creatures of far less power and excellence than himself. He envied the good that he saw coming to them and he resented their destined place. So he abandoned the life that had been laid out for him by his Maker and he determined to grasp rule and authority on his own terms. Such was his power and majesty that many among the angels followed him into rebellion, caught by the same desire for egotistical self-rule.

Corrupted now by his pride and cut off from communion with God, Lucifer degenerated into a spirit of malice and hatred. The one who had been the Son of the Dawn was now called the Evil One. He was given other names as well: the Dragon; the Serpent; Satan the accuser; the Devil; Appolyon the destroyer; the deceiver of the whole world. Hating the God whom he saw as the enemy of his proud ambition, he led his legions of angels against his Creator, attempting to wrest the throne of heaven from God by force. War then broke out in the halls of heaven. The archangel Michael led the loyal angelic armies against the Devil and, by the infinitely superior strength of God, defeated them and threw them out of heaven's realm. Satan and the rebel angels who had followed him were cast down from their high place.

Banished from heaven and the Divine presence, enchained by his own perverse choice, this once bright but now dark spirit plotted vengeance and attempted, where he could, to thwart God's plans and, if such a thing were possible, to take God's place. He and his subject angels, malignant spirits who shared his envy and hatred, now lived in the darkness of their chosen prison of self-regard. Robbed of God's reflected grace, they could think only of marring and corrupting whatever God had made, and of fruitlessly attempting to satisfy their lust for self-engorgement by subjugating others to their own darkened wills. Their abode was called Hell, Sheol, the Pit; and their existence was dominated by hatred for God, fear of each other, struggle after power, and the insatiable desire to enslave other minds.

The prophet Isaiah wrote of Lucifer's self-inflicted tragedy: "*How you are fallen from heaven, O Day Star, son of Dawn! How you are cut down to the ground, you who laid the nations low! You said in your heart, 'I will ascend to heaven; above the stars of God I will set my throne on high; I will sit on the mount of assembly in the far north; I will ascend above the heights of the clouds, I will make myself like the Most High.' But you are brought down to Sheol, to the depths of the Pit*" (Isa. 14:12–15).

Chapter 3
Material Creation and the Cosmos

In the beginning God created the heavens and the earth. The earth was without form and void, and darkness was upon the face of the deep; and the Spirit of God was moving over the face of the waters. (Gen. 1:1-2)

The fertility of God's creative thought was not ended with the creation of the angels. God went on to establish the second part of his creation, the material world. Unlike the angelic spiritual beings, who shared with God a mind and a will that could reason, decide, and love, the visible creation was to express by its variety and its extent a glimpse of the power and the beauty of the Divine Personality who brought it into being.

The material world was tied to the qualities of time and space, qualities that would both limit its operations and provide much of its beauty. Time itself began, and with it the possibility of length of years, of change, and of slowly maturing development. Space was created, allowing vast reaches of expanse within which the material world would take form. God then brought forth matter and energy, light and force. He strung out glittering galaxies and set bright stars in place; he created planets and comets and all the splendors of deep space, whose extent was so great as to seem infinite, and whose age was such as almost to defy a beginning to its time. He put the whole of this material creation into movement, its massive complex bodies as well as its microscopic particles, all whirling at different speeds and in various orbits and patterns. The angels marveled to see this new form of creation and sang for joy at its beauty and its magnificence.

Above all else the angels found joy in the complex harmonious order of all that was created. They saw in this design the workings of the mind of the Divine Son, the *Logos*, a name that signifies reason, rationality, word, and meaning. They saw that God was creating a cosmos, a patterned and purposeful universe out of what would otherwise have been a chaos without sense or significance. They saw that there was a meaning to this time-bound creation, that the coming of time meant a drama of change, the unfolding of a story, and they waited eagerly to see what the passage of time would bring about.

Eventually their attention became riveted on one small planet circling one small star, in one of the numberless galaxies spinning through space. By a rare combination of carefully ordered conditions, on this tiny bit of rock called the Earth, God added a new and mysterious quality to his material creation: he brought forth the mystery of organic life. Using the stuff of the inert material world, he fashioned through the long years ever more complex forms of life, combinations of matter that contained first an intrinsic principle of growth, then of sense, then of movement, then of emotive feeling, and finally even to the stirrings of unconscious thought. Plant life, animals, fish, birds, living things of an almost infinite variety came forth from the divine mind.

God looked at all that he had created, and he saw that it was good. The angels realized that all of material creation was moving toward a final culmination, and they understood that a new and momentous chapter in God's unfolding story was soon to come about.

Chapter 4
Man and Woman

Then God said, "Let us make man in our image, after our likeness; and let them have dominion over the fish of the sea, and over the birds of the air, and over the cattle, and over all the earth, and over every creeping thing that creeps upon the earth." So God created man in his own image, in the image of God he created him; male and female he created them. (Gen. 1:26–27)

Finally, in the slow workings of time—but what is time to time's Creator who stands entirely outside of it?—God guided his creation to its crown: he brought about a new kind of being, the human. These new creatures were a wonder to the angels looking on. The angels marveled first at their composite nature, at the way they summed up and united everything God had made. Fashioned from the "dust of the earth," they shared with lifeless matter the basic elements of its composition, its context of time and space, and its materiality. With living things they shared the quality of organic life: growth and generation, movement and sense. Most astonishingly they were given immortal souls and were gifted with minds and free wills like the angels. They were the very image of God wrought upon lowly matter, a microcosm of all creation, a small but complete universe, who in their union of body and soul, of materiality and spirit, summed up all the varied aspects of God's creative design.

God said to these humans: *"Be fruitful and multiply, and fill the earth and subdue it"* (Gen. 1:28). Unlike the angels, whose creation was immediate and entire, each separate from the other, humanity was created in two forms, male and female, who together expressed the fullness of human nature. The man was designed with the woman in view, and the woman was made with the man in mind. Again unlike the angels, the race of humans was to grow through the medium of time, and all who shared their nature were to come from this one original pair. This meant that humans were given a communal identity that was different from that of the angels; the whole human race was prefigured and in a sense present in these first two members of the race. Because of this, the individual destinies of all humans would be tied together by a close bond of essential kinship. The new race of humans was set by God upon the "slow way" to their fulfillment. Time was to accomplish their creation, both individually and as a race. They were then given the joyful task and privilege of participating in God's creative action. They were to unite with each other, physically and in a loving union of souls, and were to fill the earth with the children of their union. The angels were amazed at the high dignity God was conferring on these creatures of time and sense, whose quality of individual personality embedded in communal unity echoed the inner life of the Trinity, and whose generative potency was a participation in God's creative love.

God further dignified the humans by appointing them stewards of a portion of material creation. Just as he had brought order out of chaos, so humanity was to bring the beauty and harmony of God's order to a world in a still unfinished state. They were to "tend the garden" of the earth as they were taught by God.

Their habitation was perfectly suited to them. They lived in joy, at peace in the presence of God, in harmony with themselves, in tune with the material creation they were assigned to govern, eager for the task they had been given, and delighting in one another.

In the creation of the man and the woman, a principle deep in the mind of God was expressed, a dynamic of love and self-gift at the heart of the Trinity. The lowest would become the highest; the least would be made the greatest; the last would be the first. In the human, the lowliest aspects of creation would be raised to a height equal to the angelic beings. The angels of heaven delighted in the high place being offered to these lesser creatures and were content to enjoy and echo the love of their Creator reflected in this unexpected way.

But the sight of these happy creatures filled the Devil and his fallen angels with anger and envy. They took thought as to how they might mar God's work and destroy the destiny of this newly created race. They set about to enslave those whom they had been meant to serve and to degrade those who had been assigned such an exalted place into the lowly slime beneath their feet.

Chapter 5
The Test

The LORD God commanded the man, saying, "You may freely eat of every tree of the garden; but of the tree of the knowledge of good and evil you shall not eat, for in the day that you eat of it you shall die" (Gen. 2:16–17).

Like the angelic beings, the first humans were presented with a necessary test. They too had been granted the gift of free will: God desired children, not slaves or pets. He gave the man and woman the ability to love, to choose for goodness. They had every advantage for securing their divinely given destiny. But they could not avoid the fundamental choice: would they recognize truth and goodness and so embrace their existence as a gift from the hand of God? Or would they turn their gaze back upon themselves in pride and self-exaltation, and seek independence from the true source of their life?

Now the malice of the Devil played its part. He could not force these newly created beings to serve him; but he could attempt through suggestion to infect them with his own darkness. He knew that if they became estranged from their Maker, they would become easy prey to his own stronger will and those of his army of demons. So, he approached them and filled their ears with clever lies, trying to worm his way between them and their Creator.

The Devil laid his trap cunningly. He did not begin by tempting Eve and Adam with physical self-indulgence; he did not inflame them with an avaricious desire to amass money or possessions; he did not incite them to anger or try to set them at odds with each other. All that would come later. The trial he presented was more subtle and more dangerous, closer to their promised destiny and thus more likely to seem plausible. Adam and Eve had been given one prohibition, a warning that if they tasted of a certain tree—if they attempted to seize for themselves a certain kind of knowledge—they would be harmed to the death. Made in God's image, our first parents' likeness to God was not something they could grasp and gain for themselves; it needed to come as a gift from their Creator. The ban on eating from the tree of the knowledge of good and evil was not an arbitrary or meaningless prohibition; it was an expression of God's love for his children and a necessary caution for their survival and proper development. Yet by the nature of things it also became a test of their hearts, of the trust they had in God's intentions toward them.

Eve gazed at the fruit that had been kept from her by God's wise and loving care. She saw that it was attractive as food and delightful to the eye, and that it promised wisdom, the desire for which God had planted in her. Its appearance resonated with her own inner conviction that she was made for great, even divine, things. But instead of trusting that the same God who had lovingly created her would bring her to fulfillment and satisfy the desires moving in her heart, she listened to the deceptions of the Devil. "You will not die if you seize this fruit," he told her. "No; the opposite will happen: you will become like God!" (cf. Gen. 3:4-5). The clever liar insinuated that God was jealous of her and was keeping her from her true fulfillment. He whispered that if she would only declare independence from God and grasp her destiny for herself, she would fulfill all the greatness that she felt moving within her. This was the Big Lie, the lie that the Devil himself had first embraced, the lie that touches all free creatures at the point of their gift of freedom—which is also the point of their vulnerability.

The angels watched the encounter between the Devil and the human pair with grave interest. They knew they could not intervene by force and override Adam and Eve's freedom any more than could their dark opponent. They looked on, waiting and wondering to see what the young parents of this new race would choose, and what inheritance they would pass on to their descendants yet to be born.

Chapter 6
The Fall of Adam and Eve

We come now to a pivotal turning point in the fortunes of our race. The man and the woman had been created "very good," but their creation was not yet complete. God had given them the high dignity of participating in their own creation. He had so arranged matters that these composite creatures made of material dust and a spiritual soul would come into their inheritance as kings and queens of creation only with their own cooperation. Would they accept their creatureliness and embrace the plan of their Maker? Or would they try to create themselves according to their own designs? Would they reach out toward the truth in humility, or would they fall into the illusion of pride? Would they believe God who loved them, or would they believe his enemy who hated them? *[Eve] took of its fruit and ate; and she also gave some to her husband, and he ate* (Gen. 3:6).

First Eve and then Adam made their fateful choice. They were not forced into the choice by the Devil. It was not fated to happen by a Divine decree or by a fault of their personalities. They were genuinely free. But having once made their choice, they were not free to avoid its necessary consequences.

The first consequence of their disobedience was rupture in their relationship with God. Adam and Eve had been God's beloved children, delighting in his presence, eager to be close to the bright center of their life, walking with him "in the garden in the cool of the day" (cf. Gen. 3:8). Now when he called to them, they ran from him and hid themselves; the light of his face disturbed the darkness that had wounded them. For the first time, they knew the bitterness of guilt; they began to taste the acrid tang of corruption that their willfulness had brought upon them.

Other consequences soon followed. Rupture of relationship with God meant that the order of their lives was damaged. They were no longer at ease in one another's presence; they experienced shame and the need to hide part of themselves from each other. Further, they no longer had easy mastery of their environment; they were now forced to work hard to produce what they needed from a recalcitrant world. Their creative fertility in bringing forth the human race now involved suffering. And they found that their own inner being was no longer under their control; their minds more easily wandered into falsehood; their wills no longer settled with calm clarity upon what was good; their emotions and their senses rose up against them and tried to rule them. How could it have been otherwise? By removing themselves from their own creative source they had thrown the harmony of their being into confusion, and now they found the same disharmony spreading to the whole of their experience. All that had been ordered to their duty and their delight under the loving authority of God—creation, themselves, even the angelic order—now rose up in defiance against them, just as they had risen in rebellion against their Creator.

Most momentously, they faced the inevitable experience of death. God had *not* lied to them about the effect of their eating the forbidden fruit. Their lives had been a gift, a moment by moment sharing in God's own life that kept the mortality of their physical being at bay and vivified their minds and spirits. Like a lamp that goes out when its power is cut, like a flower that fades when taken from water, so their physical life, now deprived of its source, began to ebb away, and they heard from the mouth of God the bitter result of their rebellion: *"In the sweat of your face you shall eat bread till you return to the ground, for out of it you were taken; you are dust, and to dust you shall return"* (Gen 3:19).

Thus did the curse descend upon our first parents; and thus did they frame the legacy that they passed on to their children. Banished from their home, exiled through their own fault from the happiness that had been meant for them, Adam and Eve found themselves cast forth upon a darkened world. From this tragic pair came eventually the whole human race, a race mysteriously haunted by remembrance of what they had lost, sorrowfully aware of the height from which they had fallen: a race longing for goodness but caught by evil; desiring truth but prey to falsehood; eager for communion but experiencing loneliness; yearning for immortality but faced with the sorrowful necessity of death. The whole history of humanity, so full of promise and desire, so wracked by darkness and corruption, began to play itself out under the shadow of that fateful act of rebellion, that mysterious Fall from grace.

Chapter 7
Mankind in Trouble:
The Witness of History

A veil hangs over the exact details of our first rebellion. The loss of Eden touches on the realm of the indescribable. But its effects are everywhere to be seen and everywhere the same. The human race multiplied and spread throughout the world. When we begin to encounter what we call history, the monuments and the memories, the writings and chronicles of the peoples of the earth, we find that amid the many variations of culture and the many differences of outward characteristics, the plight of humanity is shared equally in all parts of the world. Everywhere, we find the same hopes and aspirations; everywhere, we see the same inner conflict and outer discord. Wherever humans have settled, they have brought with them their powerful talents and their incurable moral diseases. Wherever they go, they build; they fashion works of beauty and usefulness; they inquire into the world around them and penetrate many of its secrets; they aspire to the greatness that they feel within them. And wherever they go, they oppress and destroy; they involve themselves in murderous conflicts; they prey upon one another for material gain; they send up cries of suffering and succumb to thoughts of futility. And wherever they go, they die.

There is a near universal memory among the peoples of the world, often only dim and distant, of a previous golden age, a time when the burdens of existence were not intolerable, when men were wise and good. There is a near universal belief in some great deity beyond the many gods and spirits, a deity now so remote as to seem unapproachable.

And there is a near universal pattern of seeking forgiveness for moral fault through sacrificial offering, a kind of instinct for repentance and propitiation. These historical realities are oblique reminders of that terrible original calamity recounted in the book of Genesis. We become used to the fact that humans, among all animals and all other created things, are ill at ease in their existence. We find it no surprise to hear people complain of the world, or of themselves and their inner conflicts, of their terrible suffering and their desires for a better life. We understand their concerns because we experience an echo of them within ourselves. But the fact is highly surprising and demands an explanation. Why should humans find themselves so unhappy with the circumstances of their existence? Why should they need to complain about what has come through purely natural processes? Do rocks complain about their lot? Do cows long for another and better world? Do the angels of heaven fight a war within themselves, unhappy and out of sorts, unable to make sense of their lives? This befuddling predicament of unhappiness, of alienation and exile, is unique to the human race, the result of our joining the demonic rebellion and of our exile from our true home.

Our sources give us instructive accounts of our early history that indicate the results of this fall from God's favor and our desperate need for help. In Cain's murder of his brother Abel, we see that rupture with God led to disharmony and hatred between men. In the account of the Tower of Babel, raised by humans to reach to the heavens, we are presented with the characteristic human sin, the sin our race learned from the Devil: the attempt to gain divinity and eternity by our own powers. That attempt always fails, and results, as it did in Babel, in the further disruption of the human race: languages were confused and the social fabric was torn. We are told the melancholy truth that God saw and deeply regretted the evil that had infected humanity, and that he went so far as to say: *"I will blot out man whom I have created from the face of the ground, man and beast and creeping things and birds of the air, for I am sorry that I have made them"* (Gen 6:7–9).

It seemed that this grand creative project had been a failure and that the purposes of God had been foiled. It seemed that Satan had succeeded in his dark design of irrevocably harming God's creation and of enslaving the race he had been meant to serve. Yet from the beginning, from the time of the fall of our first parents, God was taking thought concerning how he would renew and re-create the human race. Would it be in keeping with God's majesty that the Devil should so destroy his handiwork? Would it be in keeping with God's goodness that he should see his creatures languishing in slavery and not do something about it? Would even an earthly king sit idly by while a great part of his country was plundered by an enemy? So God laid a curse upon the Devil—the Serpent in the garden—and gave notice of his continued concern for humanity: *"I will put enmity between you and the woman, and between your seed and her seed; he shall bruise your head, and you shall bruise his heel"* (Gen. 3:15). And though justice demanded that the human race be blotted out, in God's yet greater mercy he determined to save humanity in an unlooked-for way. After sending Noah and his sons, as guardians of the race and stewards of the world, into the protection of the Ark against the storms of destruction, God made a promise, a covenant with Noah, that he would remain with this wayward race through thick and thin, and find a way to bring them back from their rebellion and to free them from the bonds of their self-inflicted slavery.

Chapter 8
The Jews, God's Chosen

To this point in our narrative, we have dealt with matters that are by their nature beyond a simple literal account. These events—the creation of the angels and the fall of some of them, the creation of the world out of nothing and its development through long ages, the coming of the human race, and the rebellion and fall from grace of our first parents—are mighty truths, events that really happened and that touch us down to this moment. But because of their mysterious nature, they are necessarily conveyed to us in story, symbol, and mythic language. We now come to the part of our drama that enters the historical record in a more explicit way. Mythic story and historical fact begin to run closely together.

God could presumably have saved the world in any number of ways, by any number of means. He could have sent legions of angels in a counterattack on the forces of the Devil. He could have riveted the attention of the world by appearing in a majestic form in the skies, or by coming among us in superhuman shape and, attracting the multitudes by his divine beauty and power, have led us in a worldwide crusade of liberation. He could have transmitted his word to every ear or have troubled with potent dreams each one's sleep. He could have done anything he wanted. But the plan he put into motion was none of these; it was unexpected and is still thought by many to be unlikely and improbable. He chose one man—Abraham—and from that man and his wife he brought forth a people. This one people, not particularly impressive or distinguished among the nations of the earth, were to be the stage upon which God would enact the salvation of the world.

It is worth stopping for a moment to dwell on the remarkable uniqueness of the Jews. There are no other people like them; they have played a role in the history of humanity immensely out of proportion to their size or apparent significance. Even at this day, more than half the people of the world tie their deepest identity to the claims made and the traditions handed on by the Jews. Theirs has been the central religious experience of the human race. It is impossible to understand the great human drama unless we see the place in it held by the Jews. God has given them most of the decisive parts in that drama. They are the Chosen, the family singled out by God to bear the immense privilege and the difficult burden of being God's instrument for the salvation of our race.

No other people have a history like that of the Jews. It is not so much the story of a people as it is a chronicle of the deeds of God. The part the Jews themselves have played in their own history is always derivative and often embarrassingly unimpressive. What other people have kept a careful record of the ways they were unfaithful to their vocation? What other national history goes out of its way to flaunt its failures and to keep careful track of its treasons? Yet that centuries-long story of the Israelites' obstinate failure and God's unwearying faithfulness has reverberated throughout the world.

God's choice of the Jews points to certain dynamics that we will want to keep in mind as our story unfolds. In dealing with the Jewish people, God was writing the history of the human race in microcosm. What happened to the ancient Israelites was not just an interesting ethnic history, one national story among many. Their unique experience was a shadow—less substantial but easier to see—of the deeper but hidden work that God would be accomplishing among every people, and even in each individual soul. We go to the history of the Jews to see ourselves and our own history shadowed out in a kind of poetic form. As we continue our narrative, there are some interpretive keys that will help us to understand the story's true meaning.

First: God works through time. Just as he initially created the world through time, so he re-creates the world through time. He is not impressed by big numbers and splashy immediate results. God started the human race with two people, and from them, in the slow workings of time, he brought forth the many millions of humans. In the same way God initiated his plan for saving the human race with one person, and from that man and his wife—accomplishing his work over time—God has brought forth millions of *renewed* humans. Not on noisy and ephemeral mass movements, but on the hidden actions of chosen individuals the destiny of the human race turns.

Second: God operates on a communal and family principle. He does not save individuals alone; he saves families, peoples, and ultimately the race as a whole. He honors the communal nature of humanity even as he deals singly with us.

Third: God is not egalitarian, if that is understood to mean that everyone has the same experiences and the same opportunities, and gets treated the same way as they go through life. God is universally just and loving; but he deals with peoples, families, and individuals uniquely, according to his own will and his own design. He writes a different script for every character in his story.

Fourth: God prefers to work through non-obvious instruments. Abraham was not among the most powerful or the most noteworthy of the earth; the Israelites were far from being the most numerous or culturally potent people of their time, nowhere even close. Yet the fortunes of humanity were riding upon what God was doing with them.

Fifth: God often shows us the meaning of what he is doing through the use of what are called *types*, visible images that reveal in space and time the inward and invisible workings of history. Such types are real in themselves, and at the same time they are symbols of yet deeper realities, realities often only later to be revealed. Much of the history of the Israelite people and of God's dealings with them are such *types*, shadows that are awaiting their fulfillment in coming events. The whole of Israelite history unfolds like a complex musical arrangement, moving forward with purposeful tension as it seeks ever more intently for the tonic that will bring resolution to its various chords—for the realities that will fulfill the shadows that had first outlined their shape.

A final note before returning to our narrative: The children of Abraham are at the center of human history. Jerusalem is the true pole of the earth, and God has arranged matters such as to draw the whole world into their story, or to put it another way, to expand their story to encompass the whole world. Ancient Israel stands for the whole human race. Their hopes, their failures, their victories, and their defeats do not apply only to them; they stand as representatives for all of us. That is why we pay so much attention to God's dealings with the Jews as they are laid out in the sacred writings. It is their story, and it is ours.

PART II
SALVATION HISTORY BEGINS:
THE SHADOW
OF THINGS TO COME

Chapter 9
The Call of Abraham

In the secret divine counsels, God determined something like 4,000 years ago that the time had come for his direct intervention to restore a fallen humanity. The action took place in the region of the world's oldest and most developed civilizations—Mesopotamia, Egypt, and the lands between—where humans had been living in cities for thousands of years. There was a man who dwelt there in the region of Ur, an ancient city near the Euphrates river. He was a kind of sheik or tribal chieftain. His name was Abraham. God's call and Abraham's willing response set in motion the hidden divine plan that would radically alter the fortunes of the world. *Now the LORD said to Abram, "Go from your country and your kindred and your father's house to the land that I will show you. And I will make of you a great nation, and I will bless you, and make your name great, so that you will be a blessing. I will bless those who bless you, and him who curses you I will curse; and by you all the families of the earth shall bless themselves." So Abram went, as the LORD had told him* (Gen. 12:1-4).

God's call to Abraham did not involve majestic deeds or startling manifestations of power. He did not dazzle Abraham with his strength or his beauty. Instead, God made extravagant promises to him. He told him that a great nation would come from him. He promised Abraham and his descendants special protection and foretold that the whole human race would benefit greatly from his offspring. It must have been both exhilarating and perplexing for Abraham to receive these promises—and perhaps frightening, since they came at great cost. For he was required to uproot himself, leave his settled life, and take his family into an uncertain exile. With no guarantees beyond the word of God, he needed to trust: to believe that God was both able and willing to make good on his promises. He needed to put aside present comfort and security in the hope of future goodness.

Abraham's call to trust went beyond merely believing that God would take care of him in his exile. For he was already growing old, and his wife, Sarah, was beyond the age of childbearing. The promise of a multitude of descendants seemed to be incapable of fulfillment. Yet Abraham believed God, and gathering his belongings together, he left his home, taking his wife and all his household with him, and went into exile, eventually settling in the region of Palestine. By doing so, he initiated a pattern of faith, a believing response to God's promises and commands that began to undo the unbelief of Adam and Eve. Our first parents had been unwilling to entrust their future to God; Abraham reversed this sad event, throwing himself in trust upon God's goodness and mercy. He thus became the Father of all who believe God's promises and who act on them.

God was faithful to Abraham and provided well for him in his exile. He enabled Sarah to miraculously conceive and bear a son, Isaac, the child of the Promise. He made further pledges to Abraham concerning the land where he was sojourning as an exile: that it would be given to his descendants as their own. Through many difficult trials, God forged in Abraham the kind of faith that would be necessary to undo the wounds of the race.

Most noteworthy among those trials, and full of significance for the future, was God's directive to Abraham that he offer his son, Isaac, in sacrifice. To comply with this command was not only anguishing to human feeling; it meant the destruction of all the promises of future blessing. Isaac was Abraham and Sarah's only son, the one through whom the promised great nation was to come. To obey God in this instance would seem to annul all of Abraham's past obedience. It put the whole of his life—his wandering exile and his readiness to trust God's word—in jeopardy. Yet still Abraham trusted. He had come to understand God's faithful nature, and he preferred loyalty to God rather than relying on his own limited understanding.

Abraham went with his son, Isaac, to the place God had indicated and built an altar of sacrifice. "Father," said Isaac, "here is the fire and the knife for the sacrifice. But where is the lamb for the offering?" Abraham answered him, "My son, God himself will provide the lamb for the sacrifice" (cf. Gen. 22:8). He then laid Isaac on the altar. But as he was about to offer the sacrifice, God spoke to him, preventing him from doing the deed. Abraham found a ram nearby, caught by the horns in a thicket, and he offered the ram in sacrifice instead of his son. God then confirmed the promise he had made to Abraham when he had first called him into exile. *"Because you have done this, and have not withheld your son, your only begotten son, I will indeed bless you, and I will multiply your descendants as the stars of heaven and as the sand which is on the seashore. And your descendants shall possess the gate of their enemies, and by your descendants shall all the nations of the earth bless themselves, because you have obeyed my voice"* (Gen. 22:16–18).

An important encounter once took place between Abraham and a mysterious figure named Melchizedek, king of Salem. Abraham was returning from a victory over a group of local kings who had captured his nephew Lot. Melchizedek was identified as "a priest of God Most

High." Melchizedek brought out bread and wine, and blessed Abraham, who then gave him a tithe, a tenth part of all his goods. The name Melchizedek means "King of Justice," and Salem is a word meaning peace. Who was this priest of God, this king of justice and peace, who offered bread and wine along with a blessing, to whom Abraham tithed as to one greater than himself, and thus greater than all his descendants? That question would follow the children of Abraham down the long years.

Chapter 10
Jacob, Joseph, and Slavery in Egypt

The history of Abraham's descendants continued to bear meaning and consequences for God's plan to restore humanity, with all the winsome and gritty details that a family history typically contains. Abraham's son, Isaac, married his kinswoman Rebecca and by her had two sons, Esau and Jacob. As the elder, Esau should have received the Promise given to Abraham and carried it on to the next generation. But Esau was dismissive of the Promise and he despised his birthright, which in this instance meant more than just material goods or social prestige. He sold his inheritance to his clever younger brother for a hungry meal. He preferred the immediate things of sense to the invisible and future realities held out by God. So, Jacob gained Abraham's blessing and became the bearer of the destiny that God had prepared for Abraham's descendants. God then took Jacob in hand and trained him in mind and character, enabling him to win through to his true inheritance.

On one occasion, while in flight in the wilderness, Jacob was granted a mystical vision, and saw a ladder reaching to heaven upon which angels went to and fro from the invisible to the visible world. He spent the night wrestling with God as he struggled to accept and embrace the momentous call he had inherited. God then gave Jacob a new name, Israel, and renewed the promise he had made to Abraham. Jacob was later blessed with twelve sons and became the patriarch of their descendants, the famous Twelve Tribes of Israel.

Jacob had a special love for his cousin Rachel, whom he was able to marry only after working for many years. Rachel bore to Jacob the two youngest of his twelve sons. One of them, the favorite of his father, was named Joseph. The fortunes of the people of Israel, their rise, their suffering, and their further deliverance, would be tightly tied to the history of Joseph.

Joseph was greatly disliked by his older brothers. They envied their father's love for him and resented his belief in his own high destiny that he had received in dreams sent by God. "I saw the sun, the moon, and eleven stars bowing down to me!" he told them. His brothers were incensed. "So he is to have dominion over us!" they muttered (cf. Gen. 37:8-9). They plotted to kill him but at the last moment decided instead to sell him into slavery and to report him dead to his father. Jacob wept bitterly over the loss of his favorite son. Meanwhile, Joseph was taken as a slave to Egypt and was set to work in the house of a high official. There he was falsely accused by his master's wife and thrown into jail where he languished for two years. But his gift of prophetic dreams stood him in good stead with the chief jailer and others of the inmates. So it happened that when Pharaoh, the ruler of Egypt, was troubled with his own momentous dreams, he heard of Joseph and sent for him to consult about them. Joseph explained everything so ably that he was given a high post in the kingdom.

In an encounter of great poignancy, Joseph again met his brothers, who had come from Palestine to Egypt seeking food in the midst of famine. Not recognizing in this high Egyptian official the brother whom they had treacherously sold into slavery, they bowed before Joseph asking for his help, unknowingly fulfilling the dream of so many years before. Joseph recognized them and at first treated them roughly, accusing them of being spies and throwing them in jail. Then Reuben, the eldest, not knowing that Joseph could understand him, said to his brothers, "Did I not warn you not to sin against the boy? He begged us not to sell him, but you would not listen. Now this distress is coming upon us as punishment!" (cf. Gen. 42:22). Rather than plotting revenge, Joseph was overcome by affection for his brothers and the desire to see his father. After further intrigue, with comings and goings of his brothers to Palestine, he finally revealed his true identity to them. He said to his brothers: *"Now do not be distressed, or angry with yourselves, because you sold me here; for God sent me before you to preserve life"* (Gen. 45:5). Joseph then urged his brothers to go back to Palestine and to bring his father with them to Egypt, where they could be preserved from the famine that was continuing to devastate the land. They returned home and said to their father Jacob, "Joseph is alive, and he is the ruler of all Egypt!" When they were finally able to convince him, Jacob said, "Since my son is alive, I will go and see him before I die" (cf. Gen. 45:26, 28).

So, the Israelite clan, some seventy people in all, left Palestine and were welcomed into Egypt by Joseph and the Egyptian Pharaoh. They were given a choice portion of land, and there they settled and lived in peace and security for many generations. But when Joseph died and other Pharaohs who had known nothing of Joseph's history took the throne, the Egyptians began to fear this foreign people among them who had now grown very numerous. Afraid that the Israelites might turn on them in time of war, the Egyptians enslaved them and put them to hard labor. So the descendants of Abraham, the bearers of the Promise, God's chosen people who were to bless all the nations, now found themselves despised and oppressed, enslaved by a power far too strong for them to escape. Yet, the plan of God to undo the curse upon humanity was working its silent way.

Chapter 11
Moses and the Passover

Despite their grim condition as slaves, God was ruling the destiny of his Chosen. On this occasion, God raised up a great prophet and leader, Moses, to be his instrument in bringing his people to the next step in his plan of salvation.

Moses was uniquely prepared to carry out the task set before him by God. An Israelite of the tribe of Levi, Moses had escaped the edict promulgated by the Egyptians decreeing that all Israelite males should be killed. While he was still an infant, his mother, no longer able to keep him secret, gave him up to the care of God and set him floating in a small basket, like a little Ark, on the river Nile. The daughter of Pharaoh happened to be bathing there. She saw the basket and said, "Look, it is one of the Israelite children!" (cf. Exod. 2:6). She took pity on the child and adopted him as her own son. Moses was then raised in the Egyptian royal household and was given an upbringing that initiated him into the ways of Egyptian wisdom; this allowed him to deal with Pharaoh and the powers of Egypt on equal terms.

Once grown to manhood, Moses was forced to flee Egypt for killing an Egyptian whom he saw beating one of the Israelite slaves. While he was in exile in the wilderness, near a mountain called Sinai, Moses saw a strange sight: a bush that was burning but was not being consumed by the fire. He went aside to look at the marvel and was awestruck to find himself in the presence of God. God spoke to him from the midst of the bush and charged him to lead the Israelites out of their slavery. *The Lord said, "I have seen the affliction of my people who are in Egypt, and* have heard their cry because of their taskmasters; I know their sufferings, and I have come down to deliver them out of the hand of the Egyptians, and to bring them up out of that land to a good and broad land, a land flowing with milk and honey. . ... Come, I will send you to Pharaoh that you may bring forth my people, the sons of Israel, out of Egypt" (Exod. 3:7–8, 10).

Moses asked God the name by which he should be known, and God said to him: "*I AM WHO I AM.*" And he said, "*Say this to the sons of Israel: 'I AM has sent me to you. . ... The LORD, the God of your fathers, the God of Abraham, the God of Isaac, and the God of Jacob, has sent me to you': this is my name for ever, and thus I am to be remembered throughout all generations*" (Exod. 3:14–16). God explained to Moses his plan for setting his people free: Moses and the Israelite elders were to go to Pharaoh and request that the whole people be given leave to go on a three-day journey into the wilderness to worship God. "*I know,*" God told Moses, "*that the king of Egypt will not let you go unless compelled by a mighty hand. So I will stretch out my hand and strike Egypt with all the wonders which I will do in it; after that he will let you go*" (Exod. 3:19–20). Initially reluctant, Moses submitted to God's directives and, with his brother Aaron as his spokesman, went to Pharaoh and gave him God's message.

The Egyptian Pharaoh wanted nothing to do with letting the Israelites go to worship their God. He saw the probability that they would never return, leaving the Egyptians without their slaves and perhaps facing an enemy. He flatly refused. As a result, God sent plague after plague upon the Egyptians, brought about by the hand of Moses. In each case, the pride of Pharaoh kept him from recognizing and submitting to God. This violent dealing on God's part with Pharaoh had a meaning that went beyond the Egyptians and the Hebrews. God dealt with Pharaoh as a symbol and representative of the powers of the world enmeshed in the rebellion of the Devil. God had decided to act and to let both his chosen people and their enemies see his triumphant power to save.

Nothing would move Pharaoh until finally the last dreadful plague came upon him. God told him that he would send his destroying angel to kill every firstborn son in Egypt. But lest the Israelites lose their sons, too, God instructed Moses to tell the Israelites to prepare a special sacrifice.

> "*Your lamb shall be without blemish, a male a year old. . .they shall kill their lambs in the evening. Then they shall take some of the blood, and put it on the two doorposts and the lintel of the houses in which they eat them. . .It is the LORD'S Passover. For I will pass through the land of Egypt that night, and I will strike all the first-born in the land of Egypt, both man and beast; and on all the gods of Egypt I will execute judgments: I am the LORD. The blood shall be a sign for you, upon the houses where you are; and when I see the blood, I will pass over you, and no plague shall fall upon you to destroy you, when I strike the land of Egypt.*" (Exod. 12:5–7, 11–13)

So, it came about: God took all the Egyptians' firstborn sons, and in doing so "executed judgment on all the gods of Egypt." The invisible cosmic battle was being engaged through visible means. *Pharaoh rose up in the night, he, and all his servants, and all the Egyptians; and there was a great cry in Egypt, for there was not a house where one was not dead. And he summoned Moses and Aaron by night and said, "Rise up, go forth from among my people, both you and the sons of Israel; and go serve the LORD, as you have said"* (Exod. 12:30–31). So, the whole people of Israel, many thousands, immediately arose and left their homes. They took all their cattle and all their belongings, and they set off toward the desert under the leadership of Moses, not knowing where they were going or what God might have in store for them.

Chapter 12
The Covenant on Sinai

When Pharaoh learned that the Israelites had fled Egypt, he and his ministers had second thoughts. "We have behaved foolishly," they said to one another. "We have let our slaves go free at no cost" (cf. Exod. 14:5). The Egyptians gathered their army together and went after the Israelites, who were encamped in the eastern part of Egypt along the Red Sea.

The Israelites were now in great fear. They were caught at the shore of the sea, and the Egyptian army—a force they could never defeat on their own—was riding down upon them and hemming them in. At best, they would be recaptured and returned to forced labor, a condition made all the sterner because of their attempt to flee. At worst, many would be killed. The people began to complain bitterly to Moses. In a refrain that would be repeated often during the coming years, they cried to him: "Why did you land us in this terrible predicament? Is it because Egypt has no graves that you have dragged us into the wilderness to die?" Moses answered them, "Do not be afraid. Keep your ground and you will witness God's salvation. As for these Egyptians, you will never see them again" (cf. Exod. 14:11-13). Then Moses stretched his hand over the water, and God opened up a way for the Israelites to escape through the bed of the sea. Moses led them through, walking on dry ground, with the water raised like a wall on either side. The Egyptian chariot force came charging in after them. Once the Israelites had gained the other side, Moses again stretched his hand over the sea, and the waters returned, drowning the whole of Pharaoh's army. The same Egyptians who had tried to destroy the Israelites by drowning their sons in the Nile were now destroyed themselves by being drowned in the sea. And in a birth-like process, Israel was brought through a difficult passage out of water and found itself born as a people.

Freed now from slavery and miraculously victorious over their enemies, the Israelites were led by God in stages through the wilderness to Mt. Sinai, the same mountain where God had first spoken to Moses in the burning bush. What followed was an event of overwhelming importance, a decisive step in God's plan to renew humanity. God determined to make a covenant with this people, a special pact, a pledge of mutual fidelity. They would be his people, his own special possession, and they would live in accordance with the way he would teach them. God wished to dwell with humanity once again, to set up a colony of heaven in the midst of the rebellious territory now controlled by his enemy. The Israelites were to be that heavenly colony, the people among whom he would dwell and through whom he would continue to unfold his plan for regaining the human race.

The day of sealing the covenant between God and the Israelites was one of high drama. Lightning and thunder enveloped Mt. Sinai, and a thick cloud covered its heights. The mountain was convulsed by an earthquake, and smoke went billowing up from its peak. At the same time, as if out of nowhere a trumpet was heard, blasting its echoes louder and louder off the mountain's rock. Heaven and earth were being joined together in a unique moment of communion, and the divine presence convulsed the natural world. God had told the Israelites to keep back from the mountain lest they die, but they hardly needed the command. They were filled with awe and fear at the spectacle, and they drew away of their own accord. "You speak to God for us," they said to Moses. "We dare not come near" (cf. Exod. 20:19).

So, Moses went up the mountain, into the mysterious cloud,

hidden from the eyes of the Israelites, and there he stayed for forty days and nights, eating and drinking nothing. There high on the mountain God spoke to Moses as if face to face and revealed to him the glory of his goodness. Moses was so transformed by the experience that when he later came down from the mountain his face glowed with a bright supernatural light, such that he needed to wear a veil to keep the Israelites from being frightened. God spoke to Moses on the mountain concerning the way his people were to behave if he were to live among them: they would need to become holy as God himself was holy. God gave Moses a law, encapsulated in the Ten Commandments. When Moses later told the Israelites all that God had commanded, the people were united in their readiness to enter the covenant. "We will do everything God has said," they promised. Moses sealed the covenant with God by offering sacrifices and sprinkling the Israelites with sacrificial blood. As he did so, he said to them, "This is the blood of the covenant that the Lord has made with you" (cf. Exod. 24:8).

An incident took place while Moses was high on the mountain, one that pointed to the challenge the Israelites would face in becoming God's people. Moses had been lost in the cloud for many days, remote and out of sight. Down below, the Israelites, losing patience, persuaded Aaron to fashion a golden calf as an object of worship. They then claimed that this idol, made by themselves, was the divinity that had freed them from Egypt. They worshipped the false god, and then fell into the wild feasting and orgiastic behavior so common among the religions of the time. They wanted a god whom they could see and control, one who better suited their expectations and their fallen natures. Moses was warned by God about what was happening, and coming down from the mountain, he called upon his tribe of Levi to go among the people and stop the idolatrous frenzy by force. He then destroyed the idol, chastising the Israelites for their readiness to abandon so quickly their covenant with the God who had saved them. It was a sign of difficult things to come.

God spoke further to Moses on the mountain concerning the building of a tabernacle, a place of his special dwelling on earth. He showed Moses a pattern for its construction, one that replicated the harmonies of heaven. The tabernacle was to have an altar for sacrifice, and within it was to be placed the "ark of the covenant," a sacred repository where the tablets of the law would be kept. Because of the high holiness of God's presence in the tabernacle, a special order of men, taken from Aaron and his descendants, would be consecrated to God as priests to offer sacrifice and tend to the holy things. God promised that he would meet the people of Israel in the tabernacle, to live among them, to make them holy, and to forgive their sins. When the tabernacle had been completed according to the directions Moses had received, it was so potently filled with the cloud of God's glory that Moses was unable to enter. From that time forward, God made his presence known in the tabernacle as a pillar of cloud by day and a pillar of fire at night.

So it was that God made a marriage covenant with his people, wooing them in the desert, taking them as his special possession, his abode on the earth. The Promise first made to Abraham was moving another step toward its fulfillment.

Chapter 13
The Wilderness Wandering and the Promised Land

Among the lavish promises God had made to Abraham was the pledge that he would give to Abraham's offspring a land of their own, the Land of Promise. Abraham and his descendants had dwelt for a time in that land, called Canaan, but they had lived there among many other peoples as exiles and foreigners. Then had come their move into Egypt, where they had remained for many generations. When God broke the bond of their slavery and led his people out of Egypt, he made clear that the time had come for the gift of the land. Canaan was to the north and west of Egypt, some two hundred miles as the crow flies, somewhat longer as the caravan plods. It was not a great distance, even for a large group of people with their herds and flocks. Settlers crossing the American prairie in their wagons would typically travel ten or so miles a day. Even at a pace significantly slower, the Israelites should have been able to complete the journey in a few months. Yet they remained in the desert, awaiting the Promised Land, for a full forty years.

What were they doing out there in that inhospitable wilderness? Why did God lead them out of the hardship of slavery only to bring them into the harshness of the desert? The desert history of the Israelites was yet another stage in God's plan, a necessary passage if the Israelites were to complete the mission God had given them. They had now been freed from the yoke of bondage, but they had not yet understood what it meant to have God himself dwelling among them. They needed to be changed, to learn sharp lessons, to undergo a profound purification, and most importantly to come to know better the God who had called them.

Moses led them during those forty years, aided by his brother Aaron and his sister Miriam, and supported by his lieutenant Joshua. It was a difficult task. God steadily supplied his people with the miraculous bread of manna, he led them by fire and cloud, he helped them defeat various enemies that came upon them, and he lived among them in the sacred Tent of Meeting, speaking to them through Moses. Still, when all was said and done, the Israelites on the whole did not want to keep their side of the covenant. They were constantly either running after false gods, complaining about their scanty provisions even to the point of rebellion, or falling into discouragement and threatening to trudge back to the slavery of Egypt. Yet in the midst of their weaknesses and failings, God was completing a significant work among them, preparing them for the next stage of his plan.

Toward the end of those forty years, after the whole generation of Israelites who had been freed from slavery had died, Moses explained their desert wanderings to those who remained:

> *"You shall remember all the way which the LORD your God has led you these forty years in the wilderness, that he might humble you, testing you to know what was in your heart, whether you would keep his commandments, or not. And he humbled you and let you hunger and fed you with manna. . .. that he might make you know that man does not live by bread alone, but that man lives by everything that proceeds out of the mouth of the LORD. . .. Know then in your heart that, as a man disciplines his son, the LORD your God disciplines you."* (Deut. 8:2-3, 5)

God also made clear that all this discipline was for the sake of the good things he was bringing to his chosen people. He again promised them: "*The LORD your God is bringing you into a good land, a land of brooks of water, of fountains and springs, flowing forth in valleys and hills, a land of wheat and barley, of vines and fig trees and pomegranates, a land of olive trees and honey, a land in which you will eat bread without scarcity, in which you will lack nothing. . ..*" (Deut. 8:7-9).

The forty years were passed, the lessons of the desert had been learned, and the time had come to take possession of the Land of Promise. That land was indeed good and rich, but it would not simply fall into the Israelites' hands. God was battling against the dark powers of the world, and he was training his people to do battle at his side. The promised inheritance needed to be fought for, and Israel needed to be fashioned into a sword in God's hand against his demonic foes.

The land of Canaan was inhabited by many peoples. When the Israelite spies who went ahead to reconnoiter the territory returned with reports of walled cities and strong warriors, many among the Israelites grew fearful. But Joshua and Caleb, who had learned to trust that the God who had destroyed the Egyptians could handle whatever their enemies might throw at them, quieted the people's fears. The Israelites made ready to cross the Jordan river, to enter the land and engage the battles God had set before them.

Shortly before the Israelite entry into Canaan, God called Moses to himself. The great leader who had faced down Pharaoh, who had brought the Israelites out of Egypt through the Red Sea, who had spoken with God on the holy mountain, and who had guided the Israelites for forty years through many trials was not to see the fulfillment of his labors. He was buried on a mountain at the edge of the Promised Land, and there for a full month the Israelites mourned his death. But God made a promise to the Israelites, that one day he would send his people another prophet like Moses, one who would speak to him face to face, and who would lead his people out of a yet more oppressive slavery. That promise took deep root in the Israelite mind.

Just before dying, Moses spoke stern and encouraging words to the people whom he had led for so long:

> *"See, I have set before you this day life and good, death and evil. If you obey the commandments of the LORD your God. . .by loving the LORD your God, by walking in his ways. . .then you shall live and multiply, and the LORD your God will bless you in the land which you are entering to take possession of it. But if your heart turns away, and you will not hear, but are drawn away to worship other gods and serve them, I declare to you this day, that you shall perish; you shall not live long in the land which you are going over the Jordan to enter and possess."* (Deut. 30:15–18)

After the death of Moses, God established Joshua as his successor. He instructed Joshua to lead his people into their promised possession. Thus began the Israelite conquest of Canaan. Amid many battles, with the miraculous help of God who through them was conquering demonic powers, the Israelites displaced many of the previous inhabitants and settled themselves in the Land of Promise, with each of the twelve tribes receiving their allotted ancestral territory. God had made good on his promises and had proved himself faithful to his covenant. But would this people who carried the destiny of the world in their hands remain faithful to him?

Chapter 14
David and the Kingship

For many generations the Israelites lived in the Land of Promise, settling especially in the hill country away from the coastal plain. Moses had died, Joshua was laid to rest, and there was no obvious leader among them. The various tribes kept together in a loose alliance, but each tribe was occupied with its own affairs. Though the Israelites were firmly enough established in their new land, they had not been able to conquer all the Canaanite peoples. This was partly because they were regularly unfaithful to God, and so were removed from his protection. It was also, as their prophets told them, because God did not destroy all their enemies at once lest they forget how to wage spiritual warfare and so submit again to slavery.

The Israelites faced dangerous enemies external to Palestine who regularly tried to impose their rule. And within the borders of the Promised Land, unsubdued peoples also threatened their freedom. Among them were a strong and warlike people, the Philistines, who had invaded Canaanite territory from the sea and who controlled the coastlands. Spiritually it was a difficult time, a time when there was no king in Israel and everyone "did what was right in his own eyes." Again and again, the Israelites were unfaithful to God, embracing pagan idols and falling into subjection to pagan peoples. Again and again, God raised up military figures who would lead them against their foes. Thus, among others, Deborah and Barak delivered the Israelites from a Canaanite king; Gideon defeated the Midianites; Jephthah fought against the Ammonites, and Samson battled against the Philistines.

These heroic figures were the "Judges," tribal leaders who kept the Israelites from entirely succumbing to the paganism around them.

The last and greatest of the Judges was the prophet Samuel. Samuel had been consecrated to God by his mother, Hannah, from the time of his birth. From his youth he had been close to God, living in the presence of the Ark of the Covenant and hearing and speaking God's word, such that he was known and feared among all the tribes of Israel. An important step in God's plan of salvation was now approaching, and Samuel was chosen to prepare Israel for it. When the Israelites came to Samuel with a request that he anoint a ruler for them, Samuel was instructed by God to provide Israel with a king, one who would fight their battles and give them a strong identity as a nation.

This desire on the part of the Israelites for a king had a double edge to it. On the one hand, some among the Israelites were looking for the rule of God, and they wanted a king as a representative of that rule among them. This was God's desire as well, that the Israelites should have a king who would faithfully lead them and be an instrument of his protection and his just rule over them. On the other hand, some of the Israelites wanted a king so that they could imitate the nations around them, all of whom had kings, and so gain the fame and earthly glory that kings and courts displayed. They were uneasy with the invisible rule of God and restless under their unique call, and they hankered after conformity to the world's ways. So the coming of an Israelite king could be good or bad: it might be a fulfillment of God's plan, or it might mean unfaithfulness to God's rule, all depending on what the Israelites desired from their king and how the king handled his office.

God's choice for a king fell first upon a warrior from the tribe of Benjamin named Saul, who was then anointed by Samuel. Saul was a brave soldier and an effective leader; but he lacked the one quality necessary for faithful Israelite kingship: he was not careful in his obedience to the commands of God. Samuel was dismayed to find Saul unwilling to trust God for his battles and depending on human resources alone. On one occasion, when Saul had disobeyed Samuel's directives and had offered unlawful sacrifices in the hope of gaining God's favor, Samuel severely reprimanded him: "Obedience is better than sacrifice! Had you been obedient to God, he would have established your kingship forever. But now your kingdom will be taken from you and given to another. The Lord has sought out a man after his own heart to be prince of his people" (cf. 1 Sam. 13–14).

God then sent Samuel to the tribe of Judah, to the family of Jesse, among whom he was to find God's chosen king. Jesse's impressive sons came before him, each more likely than the last; but the Lord made clear to Samuel that his choice was not among them.

"Have you any other sons?" Samuel asked Jesse.

"One, the youngest," Jesse replied. "He is away caring for the sheep."

"Go and bring him," said Samuel.

When the youngest of Jesse's sons approached, the Lord said to Samuel, "This is the one!" The young man's name was David. Samuel anointed him, and from that time on, the Spirit of God surrounded David (cf. 2 Sam. 16:11–12).

While he was still a mere youth, David showed his courage and strong faith in God during his encounter with the mighty Philistine champion, Goliath of Gath. The Israelites and the Philistines were at war, drawn up in battle array, when this giant of a warrior taunted the soldiers of Saul with the challenge of personal combat as a way to decide the issue of battle. None would dare take him up on his offer despite Saul's promise of great favor for any who could defeat him. Then young David arrived, sent by his father on a visit to his older brothers. When David heard the defiant words of Goliath, he said to those around him, "Who is this uncircumcised Philistine, to defy the armies of the living God?" (cf. 1 Sam. 17:26). In his fierce love for God's honor, David came before King Saul and offered to fight the giant. David was too small to wear armor, and he was unskilled in the use of the sword. But he went up against the Philistine champion nonetheless, with nothing but a sling for a weapon. Upon seeing him, Goliath scorned him. "Am I a dog that you come against me with sticks?" Uttering curses against God, he said to David, "Come here, and I will give your flesh to the birds for their supper." But David, undaunted, defied Goliath. "You come with sword and shield to fight against the God of the armies of Israel. Today the Lord will give you into my hands, that all here may know that victory belongs to God" (cf. 1 Sam. 17:45–47). As Goliath closed for battle, David put a stone in his sling and sent it flying against his enemy. The stone struck Goliath in his forehead, killing him. David then cut off the warrior's head with his own sword, and the army of the Philistines fled in fear.

David's road to the kingship thus began with great promise. He was taken into service by King Saul and was put at the head of Israel's armies. David was a bold captain, and he won victory after victory. He formed a close friendship with Saul's son Jonathan, and he married Saul's daughter Michal. All seemed to be going favorably. But then David ran into serious difficulties. Saul grew jealous of his popularity and turned violently against him. David was forced to flee for his life into the wilderness. There he lived for many years, exiled, hiding out in deserted places with his band of picked men, or serving foreign sovereigns as a mercenary. On more than one occasion, the opportunity fell into his hands to take Saul captive or to kill him, but each time David refrained from lifting his hand against a man whom the Lord had anointed as king. Finally, it happened that Saul and Jonathan were slain in battle by the Philistines. The tribe of Judah then approached David and asked him to be king over them. So, David captured the mountain stronghold of Jerusalem and made it his capital. Within a few years he had become king of all Israel. Under his leadership, Israel's enemies were defeated on all sides, the borders were secured, and the kingdom put on strength.

David was an impetuous man whose passions often landed him in trouble and even caused him to sin gravely, a sign of the difficulty even a God-fearing man had in keeping the law of Sinai. He committed the most serious of his sins when his army was away from Jerusalem in battle, and from his palace he saw the beautiful Bathsheba, the wife of Uriah, one of his captains, while she was bathing. David had Bathsheba brought to him and had relations with her. When she later sent him word that she was pregnant, David arranged with his army commander to have Uriah killed in battle. God then sent the prophet Nathan to David with a sharp rebuke and a severe punishment for his grave misdeeds. Yet despite his sins, David's heart was with God, and his repentance was deeper than his offense. David married Bathsheba, and from her came Solomon, successor to David's throne.

David was a composer of hymns and songs, and a lover of prayer and the praise of God. He hoped to build a temple as a permanent dwelling place for his beloved Lord. He laid up great stores of timber and stone, along with immense quantities of gold, silver, and bronze. But God made it known to him that it was not for him, a warrior and a man of blood, to build his house; that privilege would be reserved for his son Solomon.

David became the archetypical King of Israel. Despite the troubles of his later years, his reign was remembered as a golden time, when God had ruled his people through his own chosen king and had defeated all their enemies. The Lord made a covenant with David, a continuation of his love for the people he had chosen and of his plan to bring humanity back to himself. God promised to David that his royal line would endure for all time, and that one of his sons would be king forever. The covenant made by God to the Davidic line of kings was treasured by the Jews down the years as a source of hope amid defeat and a promise of future glory.

Chapter 15
The Temple and the Prophets: Destruction and Exile

As David neared the end of his forty-year reign, he established his son Solomon as king after him. Solomon inherited a kingdom at peace. During his reign, the kingdom of Israel grew to its greatest splendor and extent. While still a young man, Solomon was given by God a choice as to what gift from God's hand he would most like to receive. Rather than choosing wealth or power, Solomon asked that he be given wisdom to be able to rule Israel well. The Lord was pleased by the choice, and Solomon became renowned for his great wisdom, standing at the head of a long tradition of wisdom literature that derived luster from his name.

Solomon's greatest achievement was the completion of his father David's deepest desire: the construction of a temple on Mt. Zion in Jerusalem. From the time of Moses, God had dwelt uniquely with the Israelite people in the "Tabernacle of Meeting" where the Ark of the Covenant was kept. But the Ark had been given no settled home and was vulnerable to being lost or captured. At one point the Philistines did capture the Ark of God, though they quickly sent it away in fear when a plague broke out among them. But now Solomon was erecting a fixed house for the Lord, the meeting place of heaven and earth. God was the true King of the Israelites, and the Temple was to be his palace, the place he would uniquely inhabit and from which he would rule. At the heart of the Temple was the so-called "Holy of Holies," shaped in the form of a perfect cube, in which the Ark of the Covenant was kept. None could enter that veiled and sacred place except the High Priest, once a year, when he offered special atonement for the sins of the Israelites. There was an altar of sacrifice outside the Holy of Holies where the lives of animals were offered and the blood that symbolized their life was poured out as an offering to God. There was an altar of incense where the billowing smoke represented the prayers of the Israelites going up continually in the presence of God. The Temple was to be under the authority of priests descended from Aaron and was to be kept in working order by the tribe of Levi, who were given the privilege of attending to worship, their ancestral inheritance in place of a portion of land. The Temple became the center of Israelite life and worship. It was their special glory that the God of heaven and earth, the Lord of all peoples, had made his home among them. They would sing rapturous songs about the beauty of their Temple and the joy of God's presence among them. Three times a year on the pilgrim feasts, the children of Abraham would make the journey to Jerusalem to worship God in his sacred Temple on Mt. Zion.

Though Solomon began well and ruled wisely for many years, in the end he allowed himself to be seduced by the false gods of the peoples around him. It was a sign of dark things to come. Solomon's son alienated many of the Israelites by the high-handed ways he learned from neighboring empires, and ten of the twelve tribes of Israel rebelled against him. Only the tribe of Judah, along with that of Benjamin, remained loyal to David's line. So the kingdom was divided into two parts: Israel in the north with its capital of Samaria, and Judah in the south centered on Jerusalem, a division that was to persist for two hundred years. The northern kingdom, the larger and more powerful of the two, quickly fell into idolatry. The southern kingdom fared somewhat better, but there, too, most of the descendants of David abandoned faithfulness to God and fell to imitating the pagan customs of the surrounding nations. The names of kings Hezekiah and

Josiah were remembered as faithful exceptions to a dismal pattern of unfaithfulness to God and forgetfulness of his covenant.

During this time of the Israelites' increasing unfaithfulness to their covenant, God did not forget or abandon his people. He raised up among them a remarkable line of chosen servants—the prophets or "spokesmen"—whom he commissioned to speak his word and to call Israel back to their true allegiance. From the time of Moses there had always been prophets among the Israelites who would bring God's word vividly to his people. Samuel had been one such, and the prophet Nathan had served at the court of King David. That tradition was now continued and intensified during the period of the divided kingdoms, first with the great Elijah and his disciple Elisha, and then through a long series of prophetic voices over hundreds of years: Amos, Hosea, Isaiah, Joel, Jeremiah, Micah, and Ezekiel, among others. The prophets were often opposed by the authorities whose unfaithfulness they decried, and they left behind a legacy of inspired writings along with an example of selfless service to God that would resonate down the years.

Despite repeated prophetic warnings that their unfaithfulness would bring destruction upon them, the Israelites on the whole remained stubborn in their infidelities, forgetting their covenant, disobeying the law God had given them, and imitating the pagan nations around them. Having abandoned God, they were now left without protection. A rising power in Mesopotamia, the Assyrians, invaded and put an end to the northern kingdom of Israel some two hundred years after Solomon's reign. The ten tribes were deported by the Assyrians to distant lands and were lost to history. A people of mixed ancestry were established in their former territory who would come to be called Samaritans. The southern kingdom of Judah held on for another 150 years, until they too succumbed to a new Mesopotamian Empire, the Babylonians. Many of Judah's inhabitants were taken into exile to Babylon, and their land was laid waste. Most crushing of all, the Babylonians captured Jerusalem and destroyed the Temple that Solomon had built four hundred years before. These catastrophic events threw the people of Israel into a profound crisis. God had chosen them from time immemorial as his special people, his abiding home on earth. Despite their unfaithfulness, they had never forgotten the many promises God had made them, and God had always secured a minority, a remnant among them, who had remained faithful. But where was their hope now? The Promised Land had been taken from them and ravaged by their enemies; the promised line of kings who were to reign forever on Israel's throne was deposed; the Chosen People were scattered and dispersed as slaves and exiles; and the Temple, the very dwelling of God on earth, had been pounded into dust by the pagan enemies of God.

This severe chastisement brought about a profound soul-searching among the remnant of the Jews. They pondered their past history, remembering the many ways God had led them; they considered his promises and his warnings; and they mulled over the words of his prophets. They realized that all this calamity had come upon them because of their stubborn infidelity. They experienced a new longing for the God who now seemed to have abandoned them. They yearned for their land, for their Temple, and especially for a renewal of the original covenant. *"If I forget you, Jerusalem,"* they sang, *"let my right hand wither! Let my tongue cleave to the roof of my mouth, if I do not set Jerusalem above my highest joys"* (Ps. 137:5–6). But what were they to do? Where were they to look for hope and for help? How were they to find their way back to faithfulness? How were they to worship God in a foreign land?

Chapter 16
Return and Rebuilding:
Hope of the Messiah

The destruction of the Temple and the end of the Davidic kingly rule did not defeat God's plan, nor did it destroy God's Chosen People. But it did mark a new era in their history. This was the time of the "diaspora," the dispersion of the Jews across many lands. After seventy years of Jewish exile in Babylon, Cyrus, King of the Persians, conquered the Babylonians and allowed the Jews to return to their homeland. Under the leadership of Ezra and Nehemiah, many Jews did return; they took possession of part of their former homeland and they rebuilt their temple. But now the Jews were under foreign rule, even in Palestine. Many Jews remained in Babylon or traveled to other parts of the extensive Persian Empire. Later, when the Persians fell to Alexander and the Greeks, Jews gathered in the main cities of the two Greek Empires that followed upon Alexander's conquests. The great cities of Alexandria in Egypt and Antioch in Syria became major centers of Jewish life. Populous Jewish colonies were to be found in most of the important cities across the two empires. The local synagogue took on new importance as a place of worship when so many Jews were far from their land and their Temple.

During this time of chastening and subjection, one of God's promises to the Jews took on a new and steadily increasing importance: the coming of the Messiah. From the earliest times of God's dealings with the Israelites, he had given them intimations and foreshadowings of his future plans. They had been taught, though they had often forgotten the lesson, that Israel's God was not merely a local deity but the Creator of the universe and the God of all the nations, and that Israel had a mission to all of humanity. Especially in the teaching of the prophets, they had learned that the Gentiles, the unbelieving nations, would come to know and worship the God of Israel. All the ends of the earth would hear his word; all the nations would come streaming to Jerusalem and the knowledge of God would cover the earth as water covers the sea.

At the heart of this future mission to the nations and of future glory for Israel was the promise of a coming anointed one, a "Messiah" or "Christ," who would lead Israel to the fulfillment of God's promises. At the time of the expulsion of the first parents from Paradise, God had made a promise that one of Eve's offspring would crush the head of the serpent. Later, Moses had spoken of a prophet like himself who would arise in Israel. During the period of the two monarchies, in addition to their denunciations of Israel's infidelity, the prophets had often spoken of a coming new age, inaugurated by a messianic kingly figure who would arise from the decayed lineage of David like a sprout from a dead stump and who would lead Israel to greatness, ruling with justice even the Gentiles. There was a foretelling of a new covenant between God and Israel, not like the old one made on Mt. Sinai; this new covenant would be written on the inner heart of each person. Side by side with these prophecies of glory and conquest, there were mysterious allusions to a suffering Messiah, a sacrificial figure who would save his people from their sins by taking them upon himself.

The advent of a Messiah and the coming messianic kingdom was foretold with great force by the prophet Daniel, who identified four historical empires following one upon the other. These four were eventually understood to be the empires of the Babylonians, the Persians, the Greeks, and the Romans. Daniel prophesied that during the last of the four empires, that of the Romans, God himself would establish a kingdom led by a powerful messianic figure, a kingdom that would crush all others, that would bring the whole world under its sway, and that would never end. In the midst of their disappointments, defeats, and exile, the Jews pondered these messianic promises ever more deeply. As the years passed, their hope and their longing for the coming of the Christ rose to ever greater intensity.

One series of events during this period of messianic longing, when there were no prophets and no kings in Israel, deserves special attention. The experience of the Jews under the four empires spoken of by Daniel had been a mixed one. The first of the empires, the Babylonian, had destroyed their Temple and exiled the Jews; but their Babylonian conquerors had at least allowed them to settle together in exile and to continue their common life. The second empire, the Persian, treated the Jews favorably, securing their return to the land of Israel and allowing the reconstruction of the Temple. When, two hundred years later, the vast Persian realm fell to the third empire, that of the Greeks, the Jews found themselves in the hands of two successor states, one in Egypt and the other in Syria, with the Promised Land an often contested frontier between them. The Egyptian successor state, the Ptolemaic Empire, treated the Jews on the whole well. But when control of the land of Israel was wrested from them by the Syrian-Greek Empire—the Seleucids—things went differently. One of the Seleucid Emperors, Antiochus IV "Epiphanes," demanded that everyone in his realm should adhere to the Greek way of living and of worship, by force if necessary. He attempted to impose this policy on the Jews living in Israel by forbidding circumcision and demanding pagan worship, an act that led to the famous uprising of the sons of Mattathias, the Maccabees. Mattathias raised a revolt, calling the Jews to faithfulness to the Law of Moses no matter what the cost. Through skillful guerilla-style warfare over a number of years, Judas Maccabeus and his brothers were able to wrest control of Israel from the hands of Antiochus and the Seleucids. Their daring exploits were long remembered and fueled a tradition of zealous freedom-fighting among the

Jews. Their recapture of Jerusalem and their purification of the Temple after its desecration by the Greeks is still celebrated at the Jewish feast of Hanukkah. And the depredations of Antiochus have been a symbol of the recurring threat of a darkened world's hostility toward the colony of heaven living in its midst.

The Hasmonean dynasty, as the descendants of the Maccabees were called, became kings in Judaea and were able to keep the land free for a brief period, mainly by allying themselves to the rising power of Rome. But they were not of the tribe or the lineage of David, and so could not claim to be instituting a messianic kingdom. And after a brief period of independence, a Roman general conquered Judaea and brought it under direct Roman rule. Having again tasted freedom, the Jews felt their subservience to a foreign power with bitter intensity. When the Romans tightened their grip in the face of Jewish resistance, resentment against them was fueled to a fever pitch. There were popular Jewish risings against Rome, some of them claiming to be led by the promised Messiah.

Israel was now in a ferment. Some groups of committed Jews were gathering together in communities apart—the Essenes were one such—in preparation for the Messiah who was believed to be coming soon. Others formed cadres of fighters, such as the Zealot party, who plotted to overthrow Roman rule and to regain Jerusalem and Israel by force of arms under a Messiah-general. Others, like the Pharisees, attempted to lead the Israelites into the strictest rules of priestly purity, thinking that such a purified people would be ready for the Messiah's coming. Others still—notably the Sadducees—looked for ways to accommodate the rule of the Romans for the sake of keeping the peace and maintaining the worship of God in the Temple.

All of Israel was in expectation, waiting, suffering, hoping, watching, longing, wondering: When will our Messiah come? What will be the sign of his coming? How will God establish Israel among the nations in glory? And why—oh why!—is he waiting so long?

PART III
SHADOW TO REALITY:
THE COMING OF THE MESSIAH

Chapter 17
Mary and the Angel Gabriel

In the first century of our era, when the great Augustus Caesar–Octavian–was ruling the Roman Empire, momentous but hidden events were taking place away from the eyes of the mighty and the great. All the civilized world knew the fame of Augustus, nephew by adoption of Julius Caesar, who had defeated Antony and Cleopatra, the last representatives of Alexander's Greek Empire, and had taken control of the entire Mediterranean world. All knew of his establishment of the "Pax Romana," maintained by the invincible Roman army and celebrated with incomparable majesty by the poet Virgil. Then as now, the eyes of all the world were on the important people: the brokers of power, the well-born and well-connected, the wealthy, the talented, and the fashionable. Then as now, all the world thought that it was people such as these who were molding the course of history. Then as now, they were wrong.

In a small village of Galilee called Nazareth in the northern part of Palestine, a devout Jewish couple in humble circumstances were raising a daughter, Miriam, named after the famous prophetess, the sister of Moses. Miriam, or Mary as we call her, was in her early to mid-teens, at the age when young Jewish girls prepared to marry. She was betrothed—which in Jewish society meant that a marriage had been officially contracted—to a worthy man of the town, a carpenter named Joseph. Mary was living in her parents' home, preparing to embark on full adult life. Outwardly, there was nothing to attract attention in this family circle. A poor and pious girl amid her relatives and friends, making plans for marriage and sorting out a modest life similar in its pattern to that of her parents and to countless multitudes of others, in a small town in an out-of-the-way corner of an unimportant land: not the sort of thing to gain the eyes of the great world. But inwardly, an extraordinary drama was unfolding. The most decisive event in human history was about to be enacted.

Unknown to all, even to herself, Mary had been chosen, set aside by God for a unique role in his plan to bring humanity to its true fulfillment. As preparation for that role, Mary had been secretly protected from the wound of sin carried by all the children of Adam and Eve. She alone, among the whole of the race, had come from the hand of God as if she were a new Eve, descended from her first mother in all things human, but untainted by the corruption of the Fall. Joseph, Mary's betrothed husband, was of the lineage of King David, the royal line that had been remembered and secretly treasured through half a millennium of decay. Mary, too, was of David's line. All had been preparing through long generations for the culmination of God's plan. Now the plan was to be put into action, and the angels of heaven watched with wonder as the archangel Gabriel was sent from God's presence to announce its inauguration.

Gabriel came to Mary and greeted her, not as one speaking to a common girl but as one addressing a Queen. "Hail, O Favored One, graced by the Lord!" (cf. Luke 1:28). In many Scriptural accounts of humans seeing an angel, it is noted that their first reaction is one of fear at the presence of such a mighty and unearthly being. Here we see a different response. Mary, who was never alienated from heaven's ways by sin, seems not to have been overly frightened by the simple appearance of a heavenly creature. But we are told that she was troubled by the greeting he gave her and wondered what it might mean. For one who was not corrupted by pride and who knew herself to be small and insignificant, it was unsettling to be addressed as Queen; it was troubling to be dealt with as a superior by one of the great ones of heaven.

The angel reassured her and explained the meaning of the greeting. *"Behold, you will conceive in your womb and bear a son, and you shall call his name Jesus. He will be great, and will be called the Son of the Most High; and the Lord God will give to him the throne of his father David, and he will reign over the house of Jacob forever; and of his kingdom there will be no end"* (Luke 1:31–33).

When Mary heard these words, much became clear to her. Along with the whole of Israel, she had been waiting with great longing for the promised Messiah, the Davidic ruler whose reign would never end. Along with every devout Jewish girl, she would have considered it an unbelievably high honor, the dream of a lifetime, to be chosen as mother of the Messiah. Now the angel was declaring to her just that: he had addressed her as Queen because she was to be Queen Mother, which in Israelite tradition was to bear great authority; and she was to bring forth the Promised One, the hope of Israel, the long-awaited Messiah-king. The heart of this faithful daughter of Israel leaped with anticipation at the thought. She was stirred to her depths by what the coming of the Messiah would mean for her beloved people.

But there was an obvious problem confronting her: she was not living with her betrothed husband, Joseph, so there was no means of conceiving a child. She voiced the concern, and this too the angel explained. The birth was to have an entirely miraculous origin: the Holy Spirit himself would cause the child to be conceived within her by God's power.

At this, all of Mary's concern and reserve left her. It is not unusual that someone with a special vocation will experience intimations of that calling even at a young age, in movements of soul, in unnamed longings, in desires that arise unbidden and that hold a still unidentified promise for the future. Such intuitions were no doubt part of Mary's inner life as a girl and a growing young woman, all the more so as her spirit was clear and untainted by sin. Now she saw where all those intimations, those inner presentiments and desires, had been leading. Now she realized what her sense of consecration, of being set apart for a special purpose, had meant. With all of her being she reached out to embrace the destiny God had chosen for her: "O let it be done to me just as you say!" (cf. Luke 1:38). Already her spirit was singing with joy: she had been chosen by her beloved Father for a unique destiny. He had done marvelous things for her, raised her to a place of high honor, and all nations would forever call her fortunate, blessed by God.

So, the great event that had been foretold in the holy writings began. As the Book of Wisdom had prophesied, *For while gentle silence enveloped all things, and night in its swift course was now half gone, your all-powerful word leaped from heaven, from the royal throne, into the midst of the land that was doomed* (Ws. 18:14–15). The invasion of earth by all the powers of heaven, the celestial attack upon the dark forces that had held the human race enslaved, the fulfillment of a thousands-year-old promise to undo the ancient curse, was inaugurated by the power of God and the willing cooperation of one of his creatures. The most momentous act since the creation of the world took place in the secret silence of a young girl's heart and womb.

In his love and pity for a fallen race, and in his determination not to allow Satan to defeat his plans, God had arranged for a re-enactment of the drama that had taken place in the Garden of Eden. The virgin Eve, when spoken to by a fallen angel, had in pride greedily received that angel's communication. The virgin Mary, when addressed as Queen by a heavenly angel, grew troubled and drew back in humility until she had been given confirmation of God's good purpose. The virgin Eve had disobeyed the plans of God in self-exaltation; the virgin Mary embraced the plans of God in selfless obedience. The virgin Eve had shown lack of faith in God's intentions and unbelief in his promise to bring her to fulfillment; the virgin Mary expressed profound faith in God's care and entrusted herself and her future into his hands. So, Mary, Eve's daughter, undid the sin of her mother and opened up a different path for her children. Now the human race would have two mothers and two paths laid out before them and it would be left to each to decide which of these two mothers—Mary, the humble and trusting, or Eve, the proud and faithless—they would choose to follow.

Chapter 18
The Incarnation of the *Logos*

In the beginning was the Word, and the Word was with God, and the Word was God. He was in the beginning with God; all things were made through him, and without him was not anything made that was made. . . .. And the Word became flesh and dwelt among us, full of grace and truth. (John 1:1-3, 14)

Before continuing to relate the events that followed on Mary's embrace of God's plan, it will be important to stop a moment, to attempt to understand something of this mysterious action of God and to share at least a portion of the amazement felt by the angels as they looked on, astounded by what God was doing to reclaim and exalt the human race.

It is easily enough said that in the child that was conceived in Mary's womb, "God became man." But the meaning of that short phrase has not been exhausted, the depths of it hardly pierced, by two thousand years of prayerful thought.

It would have been a reasonable expression of God's majestic rule and a sign of his merciful nature that he might intervene in human history by sending some among his loyal angels to aid the human race and to deal with the rebel angels who were oppressing them. Such an act would have been beyond human hope, but it would have had a certain fitness to it; it would have been in keeping with God's honor and nature. Yet in an act of extraordinary condescension, God chose to come and do battle for his wayward creatures himself, the Father sending his Son, the Word, to our aid. That decision alone would have conferred a tremendous importance on this lowly rebellious race. For a great King to put on his own armor and come to fight on behalf of a portion of his realm that had spurned and despised his rule would show a degree of concern hardly to be believed. Yet that isn't the half of what God actually did. Not only did he determine to fight humanity's ancient foe himself, but he took on the very nature of the race he had created, and he came among them as one of them, in a kind of veiled disguise. He who was the fountain of all existence took on the limitations of created human nature, even to the point of sharing in the consequences of sin's corruption. He who was changeless and could not suffer became a man so that he would be able to suffer for his lost children. He who was the source of all abundance took on the poverty of fallen humans so that he could make them rich. He who was Lord of life and could not die took on a mortal nature so that he might experience death in place of those who had brought death upon themselves.

It could be said that in his plan to save the human race, God faced a kind of dilemma. His problem was not one of simple power or force. God could easily crush Satan and destroy his external rule. But that alone would not save humanity. Men and women had been caught not only by the Devil's bondage but by the guilt of their own sin. Death and the Devil had power over humans because of their willing rebellion, and there were claims of justice against that rebellion that could not be ignored. Herein lay the dilemma: how was God to give these humans the opportunity of willingly turning from darkness, and how was the guilt of their sin to be justly done away with? An invasion in force might compel obedience, but that would leave humanity in the posture of the demons: hating the one they were forced to obey and facing the stern sentence that their behavior had merited. How was God to spark genuine love and faith among those who desired it without compelling their allegiance and destroying their gift of freedom? And how was their guilt to be removed? How were both mercy and justice to be rightly honored? Nothing less would serve the need.

The solution God hit upon was to take on himself the whole of humanity's destiny by joining himself to them, such that what they needed to accomplish but could not—a way to regain their innocence and overthrow their oppressor—he would do on their behalf as one of them. By this act, God forever changed the fortunes of humanity, drawing us into the very heart of the Trinity and, to use a traditional phrase, divinizing the human race. God offered humanity an entirely new start by providing a new Adam, as human as the first Adam, but now united to the divine *Logos* and extending his participation in the divine nature to all who followed him. In the words of many ancient teachers of the faith, God became man so that men might become God.

The Incarnation of the *Logos* is the most astounding belief ever (seriously) held by humans. There is no other religion whose beliefs come close to it, no other person in history who has ever claimed to be, or has ever been revered as, the fullness of the one transcendent creator-God in human form. No news so riveting and momentous has ever come to the ears of humankind. If the claim is true, if God really did become a man and join himself forever to humanity, then it is by many orders of magnitude the most important thing that has ever happened. If it is true, then the Incarnation becomes the interpretive key that unlocks the inner meaning of all human history and reveals the purpose of every human life. If it is not true, then the Christian narrative, along with the whole of the Christian religious tradition, is a lie and a cheat, and should be spurned and rejected as fanciful and dangerous nonsense.

Chapter 19
Birth, Flight, and Nazareth

The heavenly invasion of earth took place in secret, but it was not entirely unheralded. Mary conveyed the news to Joseph, her betrothed. He was initially in doubt, but the same angel who had announced to Mary the birth of the Messiah came and spoke to him and reassured him, telling him: *"Joseph, son of David, do not fear to take Mary your wife, for that which is conceived in her is of the Holy Spirit"* (Matt. 1:20). So Joseph took his place as the adoptive father of Mary's coming child. Mary's kinswoman Elizabeth was then let in on the secret. Elizabeth had conceived a child in her advanced years like Sarah, the wife of Abraham. When Mary, soon after becoming pregnant, came to visit her, Elizabeth was given to understand the identity of the child Mary was carrying. "Who am I," she said, "that the mother of my Lord should come to me?" And at the sound of Mary's greeting, the child she was carrying leaped within her (cf. Luke 1:41, 43). These two still unborn cousins, meeting in the wombs of their mothers, would have a destiny tightly tied to one another.

Mary came due at an awkward time. The Emperor Augustus had demanded that a census be taken throughout his empire, and all Jews were compelled to go to their ancestral homes to be counted for the census. The city of King David was Bethlehem, some eighty miles south of Nazareth. Joseph and Mary, being of the lineage of David, walked the distance and, having arrived in Bethlehem, found the city filled with pilgrims. They were able to find shelter only in a cave-like stable, and it was here that Mary's time came upon her and she gave birth to her child. Thus did the creator of the world enter his creation: not in frontal assault or in high dignity but under cover, unmarked, unnoticed, slipping in unseen behind his enemy's defenses. Yet neither the angels of heaven nor the devils of hell were entirely without notice of what was going on.

As to the angels, they were sent to announce the birth of the promised Messiah, not to the great ones of the world but to a group of poor shepherds sitting among their flocks in the middle of the night. It was to these simple ones that the magnificent event was announced in a vision of celestial light and music, and to them was given the privilege of being the first admitted into the presence of the newly born God-King. As to Satan and his devils, a veil was hung over their understanding, but they could still draw certain conclusions from what they saw. They noted that a group of star-gazing sages from the ancient centers of wisdom in Mesopotamia had traveled to Judea, claiming to have learned through the stars that a great king was about to be born who was sent from God. The demons feared the news, and they stirred up their servants to stop the possibility of any threat to their rule.

At the very time when God's Word was mysteriously uniting himself to humanity for our help and freedom, the warhorses of his enemies were thundering down upon him, and soldiers with drawn swords were engaged in a frantic search to find and kill him. The battle was on. Once again, the angelic messenger was sent from heaven, this time with an urgent warning: "Rise, take the child, and run to Egypt!" (cf. Matt. 2:13). The young couple fled, escaping just in time from the soldiers' brutal massacre of newborn children. They left the land of promise and traveled backward along the trail of the Israelites who long ago had been set free from the slavery of Pharaoh. This child of theirs, the founder of a new humanity whose life was to become the pattern for every life, was himself to be called out of Egypt, and to travel that same road through the desert to the Land of Promise.

What then followed was a remarkable chapter in God's dealings with humanity. The Creator was now bodily present in the midst of his creation; the author of mankind's story had entered that story as one of its characters; the majestic and infinite Being who upheld all of existence by his word of power now walked the earth as a man; and none but a select few knew anything of it.

Returning from Egypt after the death of King Herod—that representative of the corrupted world's powers whose fear and envy had forced them to flee—the young family resettled in the village of Nazareth, and there for some thirty years the child grew into mature manhood. Satan and his demons knew nothing of the fateful reckoning soon to come upon them. They had no idea that the God whom they had spurned, whose rule they had attempted to cast off at the beginning of time, was now present within their own usurped territory, disguised as a member of the enslaved race whom they believed to be securely in their power. The friends and relatives of Mary and Joseph had no notion that there was something extraordinary about this child among them, this dutiful son who worked with his father and cared for his mother after Joseph's death. He was a good man: honest, intelligent, cheerful, thoughtful, devout, respectful, a hard worker, and a valued friend. But his real identity was hidden from them.

Through Jesus' hidden years among the people of Nazareth, God imparted a special dignity to the quiet existence of the vast majority of those he had come to save. He honored them by sharing the small details of their lives: their hard work and careful economy, their joys amid struggle and their hopes amid grief, their aspirations and anxieties for themselves and their families, their tragic sense of life's flowering and decay—the whole experience of a race longing and suffering under the ancient curse.

Yet this time of quiet and unobtrusive living was preparing the world for a great cataclysm. For this child had been assigned the name of Joshua—Jesus—a name that means "God saves," after that great leader who had battled Israel's enemies and brought them into the Promised Land. This greater Joshua was eager for the day when the prophecy implied in his name would be fulfilled. The time was approaching when the eternal Son would take up his Father's business; when the long-awaited Messiah-king would reveal his identity to his people; when the battle foretold from the beginning would be hotly joined. The angels looked on in wonder, watching and waiting.

And then a voice, piercing earth and sky, arose like a trumpet blast from the desert of Judea, riveting the attention of all Israel: "The time long foretold has arrived! The Lord is near! Prepare yourselves for his coming!" (cf. Matt. 3:1–3).

Chapter 20
Jesus Begins His Mission

In the last verse of the last book in the Hebrew scriptures, that of the prophet Malachi, written some five hundred years before the birth of Jesus, God had made a promise to Israel that was hanging in the air: *"I will send you Elijah the prophet before the great and awesome day of the Lord comes"* (Mal. 4:5). Now that prophecy was being fulfilled.

The piercing voice from the wilderness that was shaking all of Israel belonged to John, the cousin of Jesus who had leaped in the womb of his mother so many years before. John was the forerunner of the Messiah, and his pattern of life bore a striking resemblance to the one whose coming he had been called to prepare. John, too, was miraculously born, with significant prophecies at his birth concerning his future. His early life was hidden, but as a grown man he began preaching in the desert, quickly becoming renowned and revered as a prophet, not only in Israel but among the communities of the Jewish diaspora. He preached the coming Kingdom of God, and he called his hearers to repentance. He gathered a group of disciples around him, baptizing those who came to him. John's ministry made a deep impression on those who saw and heard him; all of Israel seemed to be going out to him in the desert, hanging on his words. Many thought that he was the Messiah, or the Prophet promised by Moses. He insisted that he was not, that his task was to prepare Israel for that Coming One. As his popularity and influence grew, so did opposition from some of the Jewish authorities. Finally running afoul of the royal family because he denounced their illicit marriage, he was imprisoned and, after a time in captivity, shamefully executed. By the shape of his life, by his preaching and baptizing, and by the manner of his death, John was shadowing out the life of the Messiah and was preparing Israel for the mission of their true king.

When the time came for Jesus to begin his assault on the Devil's stronghold, his first act was to go to John in the desert and to be baptized by him. John represented all that was best and truest in the Jewish tradition. By receiving baptism from John, Jesus embraced the whole of that long history, placing himself squarely within it and pointing it to its fulfillment. As Jesus was baptized, John was given to see the Holy Spirit descend upon him and to hear the voice of the Father from heaven declare: *"This is my beloved Son"* (Matt. 3:17). God in his fullness was present, now united to humanity in a new way, and John knew that his task had been completed: the "bridegroom" had come, and the friend of the bridegroom needed to diminish and depart. John spoke reverently of Jesus to his disciples, pointing him out as the lamb of God, the sacrificial offering that would fulfill the sacrifices of Abraham, the Passover lamb, and the offering of Moses at the sealing of the Covenant on Sinai. Some of John's disciples attached themselves to Jesus and became his close followers and friends.

Soon after he had been baptized, an act that signaled the beginning of his messianic mission, Jesus was led by God's Spirit into the wilderness for the first round of his hand-to-hand combat with Satan, the one whose rule he had come to contest. For forty days, mirroring the Israelites' forty years of purification in their wilderness wanderings, Jesus was assailed by the Devil's most potent attack against humanity: namely his lies and seductions. The first Adam had succumbed to that seductive voice and had believed the lies of the Devil; but now the new Adam, the founder of a renewed humanity, responded to Satan's subtle attack with defiance toward him and faith in God. As Mary by her faithfulness had begun to undo the sin of Eve, so Jesus by his loyalty to the Father yet more decisively undid the sin of Adam. Satan was baffled and humiliated. He was confused by this Israelite, this son of Abraham and David. He saw Jesus to be a mortal man, descended from Adam and a member of a fallen race. He was confident in his power over all the members of that race; yet this man strangely eluded his influence and threw back his assaults. So, the enemy of mankind drew off, biding his time, waiting for a more propitious moment.

Now returned from his secret desert battle, Jesus set about establishing his Kingdom. The first task was to gather a group of disciples who would constitute the spiritual foundation of the new Israel, twelve men to match Jacob's twelve sons. Among the disciples of John the Baptist was a Galilean fisherman named Andrew. In Andrew's excitement at meeting Jesus, he sought out Simon, his brother, and told him, *"We have found the Messiah!"* (John 1:41). Andrew brought Simon to Jesus, who gave him a new name: Peter, the Rock. Peter was to be the lead man in Jesus' Kingdom, a key foundation stone for a renewed humanity. Jesus then chose others to complete the company of the Twelve Apostles. Along with Peter and Andrew, there were another pair of brothers, also fishermen, James and John. Jesus had a special love for these two fiery brothers, nicknaming them the "sons of thunder." Two other Galileans were chosen, Philip and Nathanael. There was a tax collector named Matthew, a man of the Zealot party named Simon, a relative of Jesus named James; then Thomas, Jude, and—momentously—Judas Iscariot, who would later turn traitor. Jesus invited the Twelve to live with him, to join him in his work, and to carry on building the Kingdom in his name once his unique earthly task had been accomplished. As a group, the Apostles were not an especially imposing set. They were a diverse, even motley, crew of men, of a sort one might find almost anywhere—not uniquely well-educated, not socially powerful, not particularly talented. They were hardly the kind of people to set on foot a potent movement of historic importance and worldwide influence. It was clear from its beginnings that the Kingdom Jesus was building would not be established through human talent or power alone. If it were to grow and gain influence, it would do so by God's sovereign action, working through normal and often unimpressive channels of human life and energy.

Chapter 21
The New Moses

As Jesus undertook his mission, he had a delicate task to perform. He was coming to Israel as their Messiah, the long-promised anointed one; but the people to whom he was coming had mistaken notions as to who the Messiah would be and how he would act. Their reading of the ancient prophecies had led them to think that the Messiah would be a king after the fashion of David, only on a much larger human scale. David had been a great fighter, a warrior who had battled and defeated Israel's enemies and secured for himself a powerful throne. In the same way, the Messiah would raise a military standard and lead the Jews against their enemies, calling his people back to faithfulness to the Covenant, establishing them in freedom, and going on to conquer a great empire in the name of God. How this messianic understanding fit with the prophetic picture of a suffering and sacrificial Messiah was not clear. Some thought that such dark prophecies did not refer to the Messiah at all but to Israel as a whole. Others conjectured that there might be two Messiahs, one suffering and one victorious.

Jesus thus needed to reveal himself as Messiah, as the one who would bring about the promised Kingdom, while at the same time teaching Israel the true nature of that Kingdom, which was to be fundamentally different from what most of them expected, a Kingdom "not of this world." He needed to negotiate the highly volatile messianic hopes in the air that could easily lead into mistaken and even dangerous and bloody channels. It is clear from the Gospel accounts how carefully he went about his business. At times, he kept the knowledge of his messianic identity secret. At other times, he acknowledged that identity but quickly recast its meaning. At still other times, he spoke and acted boldly in ways that made clear his messianic claims. At all points, he was master of events, not allowing himself to be shuffled along or manipulated by false expectations of whatever kind.

In revealing himself to Israel, Jesus took upon himself the identity of a recognizable Jewish figure: that of the prophet-rabbi. The long Jewish tradition had made such a figure both revered and turbulent, as the recent history of John the Baptist had shown. To gather a group of disciples together, to live with them, and to teach them the ways of God was what rabbis—teachers of the law—customarily did. To go from town to town and engage in public preaching and prophetic action was rarer, but it was in keeping with a venerable prophetic tradition. None of this was strange or shocking to the Jews. Those who heard Jesus, or heard news of him, thought him to be a prophet like Elijah, Jeremiah, or John the Baptist, and his own followers often called him Rabbi. What made Jesus so arresting to those who heard him—either thrilling or disturbing depending on how one judged it—had to do with the manner of his teaching and the evident power of his actions. All were astounded by the authority with which he spoke and acted, especially for one who had received no formal training. He was a rabbi, yes, but not like other rabbis; he spoke in an entirely different key. He was a prophet, true, but seemingly more than a prophet, because he often seemed to be speaking not in another's name but in his own. By what he said and by what he did, Jesus continually provoked the question in the minds of all who saw and heard him: "Just who does this man think he is?" It was exactly the right question to be asking.

An example of the boldness of Jesus' prophetic stance can be seen in the core body of his teaching that has come down to us as the "Sermon on the Mount." Jesus ascended a height, as Moses had done, and from that height he delivered a law. To his Jewish hearers, so well-versed in the Scriptures, it was evident that he was claiming by this act to be the Prophet promised by Moses and to be handing down a new law, one that in Jesus' own words would not abolish the law given at Sinai but would fulfill it. If this were not bold enough, Jesus spoke of this new law as if he himself were its source. There was no Exodus-like drama here of God resting on the top of the mountain in fire and thunder and the prophet Moses going courageously up to meet him, the Israelites meanwhile cowering in wonder beneath. Instead it was Jesus himself who occupied the mountain, and his disciples were gathered there with him. He then delivered the new law with breathtaking authority. Not "Thus says the Lord," as the prophets had spoken, but instead, "You have heard it said. . .but *I* say to you. . ." This was the decisive formula that lay behind the whole of his teaching. It astonished and troubled those who heard it.

The moral content of Jesus' teaching was in keeping with Jewish law and tradition, yet he consistently raised the stakes and deepened the demands of that law. The Jews had been taught to love their neighbor; now Jesus insisted that they go further and love even their enemies. The Jews knew that it was wrong to take another's life; Jesus taught that they were not even to speak against others. The Jews knew that they should act toward others with justice; Jesus told them that they should take no revenge for offenses and should forgive those who did evil. The Jews were aware that adultery was an affront to God and an act to be carefully avoided; Jesus told them that even thinking about it privately would lead to judgment. It had been hard enough to keep the moral precepts of the law given by Moses—hard, but still remotely possible. But this new teaching of Jesus seemed simply impossible: *"You, therefore, must be perfect, as your heavenly Father is perfect"* (Matt. 5:48). How was that to be obeyed? The teaching of Jesus necessarily implied something further: it demanded a fundamental change in the inner moral being of his hearers such that what was previously impossible would become possible. Jesus was telling earth-bound creatures that they needed to learn to fly. If this were not to be mere idealistic fluff, it would demand in Jesus' followers the growing of wings; it pointed to a qualitatively different kind of law, one that would take root in each person and transform the faculties of the mind and the will. It assumed divine power for a radical change of heart.

Such bold teaching was difficult to take seriously. It could seem the result of a mistaken or even a deluded mind and liable to be shrugged off as unworthy of serious notice. And so it might have been, except for another quality displayed by Jesus. He not only spoke with great authority, which was perhaps easy enough to manage, he also accomplished deeds of astonishing power that left his onlookers frightened, amazed, and exhilarated by turns.

Chapter 22
The Authority of Jesus

Authority is a word close in meaning to the word "author." It was fitting that the one who had authored the story of the human race, and who had now entered that story as the world's savior and king, should be seen to possess authority. But Jesus was not merely to speak with authority. His deeds corresponded to his words. He quickly gained the reputation of being a wonder-worker, a man around whom miracles sprouted on all sides. Yet there was a special quality to the miracles and acts of spiritual power performed by Jesus. There was nothing of the atmosphere of the magician or the wizard about him. He did not fly through the air, or cast spells, or make things appear and disappear, or change himself and others into strange shapes. There were no dazzling displays of fire and light spinning from his fingers, no arbitrary manipulations of matter to amaze and impress crowds. All his miracles possessed a quality fitting for the author of creation. They were deeds of love, compassion, healing, judgment, and governance, in keeping with the rhythms of the created order, setting right what had been corrupted or destroyed.

Wherever Jesus went, he physically healed many who came to him. The blind were able to see again; the deaf could hear; the lame walked; the crippled could again use their limbs. He who had created the world was restoring heavenly order to a region that had fallen into chaos. Wherever Jesus went, he cast out demons with a word. He had come to end the usurping rule of the fallen angels, and he showed his authority over them by sending them fleeing. Wherever Jesus went, he healed leprosy, a symbol of the guilt of sin, of humanity's impurity in the presence of God. Lepers were held by Jewish law to be unclean, and those who touched them caught their uncleanness by a kind of contagion. Yet when Jesus touched lepers, the contagion worked in the opposite direction: instead of him becoming soiled, they caught his purity and were cleansed. It can be imagined what kind of effect this had on the people of the villages and towns Jesus visited. They flocked to him by the thousands, bringing their sick, their leprous, all those possessed by demons, hoping for a cure. The numbers grew so great that in a short time Jesus could no longer walk about openly lest he be mobbed by crowds.

Of particular amazement to the Jews, and of great perplexity to the demons, was Jesus' occasional act of bringing a dead person back to life. Death had been the most grievous consequence of Adam and Eve's sin, the strongest hold of Satan upon humanity. It was the deepest humiliation of the race, the blot that darkened all of human life, the destination that withered all hope, the sure sign of slavery to the devil. Yet here was a man, a mortal son of Adam, who seemed to possess authority even over death. People marveled that God had given such authority to a man. And again, the question was forced upon the onlookers, both human and demonic: Just who was this person? How did he come by such authority that even the demons were forced to obey him and the dead came back to life at his word?

As striking and provocative as were his miraculous works, Jesus always made clear that they pointed to deeper, hidden realities. The divine *Logos* did not enter humanity only in order to eradicate the immediate effects of physical disease for a few people during a brief span of time. He was pursuing the ultimate spiritual cause of all physical frailty. His acts of physical healing were signs of a more profound healing of the soul. He needed to teach his hearers the realities of the invisible world, to help them understand the real nature of their slavery and their poverty. So he performed visible signs that would catch their attention, but he would then direct their gaze to the invisible truths to which they pointed and upon which everything hung.

A telling example of these priorities can be found in the account of Jesus healing a paralyzed man. Jesus had been preaching to a packed house when a paralytic was brought along by friends, hoping for healing. Finding no way to enter the house due to the crowd, they opened a hole in the roof and lowered the man down on his pallet. Jesus, whose sight encompassed the whole of reality, saw into the man's soul and recognized in him a person who wanted to return to faithfulness. In his compassion, he immediately reached out and touched the man at the point of his cruelest suffering and deepest need, saying to him, *"Take heart, my son; your sins are forgiven"* (Matt. 9:2). The divine doctor perceived and healed the real condition that was weighing upon his patient, his burden of guilt. When some of those present began to grumble, thinking that this showed blasphemous presumption on Jesus' part, he said to them: *"For which is easier, to say, 'Your sins are forgiven,' or to say, 'Rise and walk'? But that you may know that the Son of man has authority on earth to forgive sins"*—he then said to the paralytic—*"Rise, take up your bed and go home." And he rose and went home* (Matt. 9:5–7). Jesus performed the relatively easy act—for him—of visibly healing the man's body so that his hearers would know that he had the power to perform the far more momentous and hidden operation of healing the mortal wound in his soul.

Chapter 23
The Opposition Grows

It was not long before Jesus became the center of serious contro-versy among the Jews. Much of the positive public sensation he created was the result of the miracles he performed. But there were other rea-sons why Jesus won his way into people's hearts, especially among the poor and the socially insignificant. He had an evident love for those in humble circumstances. The needy and the downtrodden found in him a sympathetic ear and a decisive advocate. He was a person with wide human sympathies. He could be found weeping over the death of a friend or leaping for joy at the grace of God among his disciples. His eyes would flash with indignation at falsehood, and he could spring into action at irreverence in the Temple. He could read people's hearts, and he often spoke with homespun irony and an evident twinkle in his eye. He was a spellbinding teacher who knew how to clothe the deepest truths in short and dramatic sayings and stories. At the same time, he would never play to a crowd or court the good opinion of his hearers.

Just when it seemed that all were pleased with him, he would speak hard truths and make rigorous demands. He united a profound con-cern for his hearers with an unflinching seriousness about truth and justice. The combination was hard to resist. Despite his high moral call and his constant urging of the need for repentance, even hardened sin-ners—prostitutes and tax collectors—sought him out. It was therefore not surprising that after an especially powerful miraculous act, when Jesus had fed five thousand people in a deserted place, multiplying a few loaves of bread into rich abundance and thereby evoking manna in the desert, those who witnessed the miracle rose up and attempted to enthrone him as their Messiah-king. Could anyone claiming to be the Messiah do more than he had done? Could anyone show more evident signs of God's favor? Had anyone ever spoken or acted like this man before? He must be the One for whom we have waited so long!

If this were the whole of what Jesus had said and done, it would be hard to understand why his messianic bid was anything but successful among the Jewish people. Some level of resistance to moral and spiritual reform might always be expected. But Jesus was so obviously the opposite of a moral hypocrite, so genuinely concerned for the welfare of his followers, and so impressive at backing up his words with deeds of power that his success should have been assured. Yet there was another current in the words and acts of Jesus that was hard for many of his hearers to come to terms with, especially for those most educated in Jewish law and tradition. It was not his moral teaching that got him into trouble with such as these; it was not his miracles they mainly objected to. It was rather the idea, one that grew stronger and more unmistakable as time went on, that this man, this rabbi, this prophet, was making claims about himself and his mission that no mere man could possibly claim.

What was one to make of a man who said not only that he was greater than David, Solomon, and Jonah—an audacious enough claim—but that he was lord of the Sabbath day? The Sabbath observance was part of the holy law given by God himself. If Jesus had only offered a new interpretation of the Sabbath, he may or may not have been agreed with, but he would have shown himself to be a customary rabbi, commenting on and submitting to the Jewish law. But Jesus was claiming to be superior to the law and to have the personal right to pronounce upon its true meaning. What could that mean? And what was one to do with a man who claimed the authority to forgive other people's sins, not committed against himself? What was to be thought about a teacher who said not only, "I will show you the right way, and I will teach you the truth, and I will point out the path of life to you," but, shockingly, "I *am* the way, I *am* the truth, I *am* the life" (cf. John 14:6, emphasis added). What was one to think of a man who made personal loyalty to himself the measure of all goodness, in claims like: "He who loves father, mother, sister, brother, more than me, is not worthy of me," and "He who does not hate his very self cannot be my disciple"? (cf. Luke 14:26). Could it be that he was claiming to possess the authority of the God of Abraham, Isaac, and Jacob, the creator and lord of the universe? Could it be—impossible thought!—that this man who ate, and drank, and spoke, and slept like any other man claimed in some mysterious way to *be* God?

Jesus carefully adapted his self-revelation to his hearers' spiritual maturity so as not to overwhelm them all at once, but eventually he left no doubt about his meaning. "I tell you most solemnly," he said publicly: "Before Abraham was, *I am*" (cf. John 8:58, emphasis added). *"I and the Father are one"* (John 10:30). In the face of such claims, and after witnessing such extraordinary miraculous signs, there were only two reasonable responses that those who saw and heard Jesus could make. Enlightened by heavenly help, they could say with Peter: "You are the Messiah, the Son of the Living God!" (cf. Matt. 16:16). Or, with minds closed to God's action and wills hardened by pride, they could say with some of the Pharisees: *"He casts out demons by the prince of demons!"* (Matt. 9:34). Whatever else Jesus may have been, it was clear to those who encountered him that he was not simply a man like other men, a teacher and a prophet to be honored, opposed, or ignored according to a human scale of understanding. This person was either God himself, mysteriously come among his creation in the form of a man, or he was the Devil incarnate, exercising superhuman powers through demonic agency. There began to form around Jesus two camps: those who had experienced the presence of God through the veil of his humanity and who worshipped him as no mere man should be worshipped, and those who stiffened in their resistance to God's presence in him and sought to eliminate that influence, and if possible to put him to death. It was a pattern that would repeat itself in every time and in every human heart down the ages.

Chapter 24
Jesus Announces the Gospel of the Kingdom

When the angel announced the birth of Jesus to the shepherds, he is reported as saying: *"I bring you good news of a great joy which will come to all the people; for to you is born this day in the city of David a Savior, who is Christ the Lord"* (Luke 2:10–11). "Good news of great joy": the Greek word *evangelion*, translated into English as Gospel, means "good news" or "glad tidings." It was used by officials of the time to announce important events: the winning of a great battle, the enthronement of a new emperor, or, as in this case, the birth of a royal heir. Jesus used the same term to describe the core of his message: the good and joyful tidings he had come to announce. From the beginning of the establishment of his Kingdom, preaching the Gospel, announcing the Good News, was at the heart of Jesus' mission. Wherever he or his followers went, the announcement was made that the Kingdom of Heaven was at hand. What were some of the key elements of this Gospel, the glad tidings of the kingdom, that Jesus brought to the human race?

The first and perhaps greatest "news item" was the simple fact of God's continued interest and presence in human affairs. Prisoners languishing in an enemy jail gain courage to find that their plight is known to their own countrymen and that steps are being taken on their behalf. Likewise, a race languishing under the curse of death and the rule of Satan were overjoyed to find that God had not forgotten them. All the more intense was their joy in hearing that he had not only taken pity on their misery, but that he himself had come among them to do battle on their behalf and to free them from their slavery; that they were not only remembered but loved and desired, and that careful plans for their future happiness, long in the making, were soon to be brought to fulfillment.

Another key announcement of the Gospel was the news that God was ready to forgive the guilt of any who requested it. There was a stern judgment coming upon the world, upon its demonic rulers and their human allies, and justice would be done to the guilty. But before the arrival of that fateful day, a reprieve was offered; a kind of general amnesty was declared for any who had been caught in the Devil's snare. Peace was proclaimed between heaven and humanity; past misdeeds would be forgotten, and any who wished could claim the pardon. So great was the desire of the heavenly Father for his lost children that he was ready to go to all lengths to find a way to blot out their sins, no matter how evil they may have been. The burden of guilt that had lain so heavily on human consciences was to be lifted, and the just sentence upon rebels and doers of evil was to be transferred from them and carried by God himself.

Not only were dark deeds to be forgotten and guilt remitted, but there was promise of a new healing power from God that would enter the heart and soul of each person reconciled to heaven. The searing self-inflicted wound that had darkened the minds and wills of the race and had given them a propensity to evil would be addressed and its healing begun, and a new capacity for goodness and truth would be engendered, along with new powers of self-mastery and love. The fulfillment of the ancient prophecy of a new Covenant according to which the ways of God would be written on the human heart was now to be inaugurated.

It was announced that the enemy of mankind, that malicious spirit whose lies had first seduced humans to slavery, was to be defeated and his rule overthrown. The strong bars of Satan's prison were to be rent open. Humanity was to be set free that they might live as they had been created to live, in union with God, at peace with one another, and in harmony with the rest of creation.

It was declared that the most terrible consequence of humanity's guilt and Satan's slavery, death itself, would be overthrown. The humiliating embarrassment of the grave would be forgotten and death would be no more. The decree of banishment from Eden was to be reversed, the curse was to be lifted, the long exile was to be ended, and a lost and wandering race was to be welcomed home.

As if all this astounding news were not enough, it was proclaimed that all these gifts were to be accompanied by an unimaginable grace: humanity was to be made divine. Mere men and women were to be given a share in the very nature of the Eternal God, raised to a height among the angels of heaven themselves, and adopted into the endless cataract of love called the Trinity.

Such were the stupendous tidings Jesus announced, the best and most thrilling news ever brought to a suffering humanity. Yet there was a high cost involved for any who wished to embrace the offer. First, those who were touched by the grace of God and wished to receive the reconciliation with the Father offered by Jesus needed to repent of their sins. They needed to acknowledge their past rebellion, sue for forgiveness, and change the direction of their lives. They had to recognize both the evil and the futility of declaring themselves independent from God, and return in faithfulness to their rightful king. Second, they had to utterly renounce their allegiance to Satan, the prince of lies. They had to break with his kingdom and to withdraw themselves, by God's strength, from the web of seductive darkness that Satan had woven around humanity. In doing so, they would inevitably bring upon themselves Satan's anger and malice, and they would need to be ready to confront and endure whatever his enmity threw at them. Third, they needed to learn to live in a manner befitting their new status as divine creatures. They were to imitate the ways of heaven so that they might be worthy to live among the angels and in the presence of God. With divine help, they were to undertake the hard task of remaking their hearts and of learning new loves. They were to become masters of themselves and their desires, to love one another from the heart, to treat each other justly, and to imitate the forgiveness and forbearance of their heavenly Father. They were to renounce pride and vanity and learn the ways of humility. They were to put their former selves to death and become new creatures, members of a regenerated race. In imitation of their Master, and supported at every step by his grace and power, they were to walk the lowest of roads to reach their destined high place.

By a measure that dignified humanity beyond telling, God arranged that it was a man who would accomplish all these great deeds on behalf of humanity. A man would battle Satan and throw him down. A man would bear the sins of his fellows and cancel their guilt. A man would gain for his brothers and sisters the gift of eternal life. A man would lead humanity into the very heart of the Father. A man who was also mysteriously the eternal Son of God.

In order that this proclamation of freedom might be announced across the globe and down the generations, the Kingdom of renewed humanity under the rule of the Messiah was not to be established in its fullness right away; instead it would take root in the midst of a fallen race. And like a resistance movement against the dark spiritual powers ruling the world, it would continue the fight for humanity through the years. The Savior-King would spiritually inhabit his newly regenerated brothers and sisters and teach them how to announce the Gospel and how to wage spiritual warfare for themselves and for others, such that each might bear a portion of the honor of defeating the enemy and winning a place in the Kingdom. The battle would be fierce: against the Devil, against the forces of evil in the world, and against the dark wound in each soul. It would demand a total commitment, even at times to the shedding of blood. But God would be with his followers, giving them strength and joy in the fight, and assuring victory to those who remained under his protection.

As might be predicted, a message of this kind evoked a strong response. Wherever Jesus and his disciples made their proclamation of the Good News and gave miraculous signs of its truth, they threw their hearers into a tumult. Some were overjoyed; others perplexed and amazed; still others angry and troubled. None were left unmoved. The Father, in his son Jesus, had come among his creatures to call them back to their true loyalty and to give them the power to throw off the chains of their slavery. As Moses had done before him, yet with deeper meaning and infinite authority, Jesus set before Israel life and death, blessing and curse. He led all who saw and heard him by stages to a point of inevitable choice. By that choice, they would determine their destiny.

Chapter 25
Jesus Marches on Jerusalem

The duration of Jesus' public mission was something like two or three years. He spent the majority of that brief time preaching in the northerly region of Galilee and in territories nearby. Occasionally he visited Jerusalem and its surroundings, especially for the Jewish pilgrim feasts. But opposition from the authorities meant that it was dangerous for him to spend much time in Judea or Jerusalem.

There has developed in some quarters a romantic picture of Jesus as a wandering rabbi traveling from town to town in haphazard fashion, preaching an idealistic message, stirring hearts and minds and then moving on, eventually somehow finding himself in Jerusalem where he ran into serious trouble and was put to death. But the reality was quite different. Jesus was following a careful plan of action. He was purposeful and strategic in all that he did. Among the many human talents he displayed, Jesus was an excellent organizer who knew what was required to establish a society that would be effective for his messianic mission and that would endure through time.

The Gospel accounts do not give much space to what might be called the organizational and strategic side of Jesus' activity, probably because it was evident and taken for granted by the early believers who wrote and passed on the accounts. But they do give us certain details that allow us a glimpse of the significant level of planning and organization that lay behind Jesus' mission. A few examples of that gift in action can help fill in the picture.

- As Jesus went from place to place preaching, he typically brought with him a substantial company. The Twelve Apostles were present, along with other disciples; a group of women handled food preparation and other material needs, among them, notably, the wife of King Herod's steward. The exact number of this ordered traveling company is not given, but it was at least a few dozen, and seems often to have been many more. Its members would all need to have been fed, clothed, and housed as they went along. There were no signs of vague disorder in their life together. All was well planned and well managed.

- Jesus set up his base of operations in Galilee, apparently in the town of Capernaum, the village called in the Gospels his "home." He and the members of his company regularly set out and returned again to this base camp as the campaign unfolded.

- The Twelve Apostles were given specific tasks for the common effort. Peter occupied a position of leadership among them. Along with him, James and John seemed to have special roles, and they accompanied Jesus at important times. We are told that Judas was the treasurer of the company. At one point, Philip and Andrew were approached by some men who wanted to speak with Jesus, the two Apostles acting as attendants upon a king dealing with those seeking an audience.

- At a certain stage in the campaign, we are told that seventy men were tasked with preaching the Gospel, two by two, in the towns Jesus was planning to visit. These men would have had to be identified, initiated into the company, and trained. Each of the thirty-five pairs would have had specific marching orders. It was evident that Jesus had a predetermined strategy for his preaching mission. Anyone who has ever been responsible for this kind of coordinated activity knows how much planning had to go into the effort.

- When Jesus performed the wilderness miracle of feeding the five thousand, the account notes that he had all the men seated in groups of fifty before feeding them. This was Israelite battle array and bringing a crowd of thousands into that kind of order would have been no simple task; it would have demanded careful coordination and management.

Part of the stiff opposition Jesus provoked arose from the realization that he was putting together an effective movement imbued with clarity of purpose and a plan of action. Solitary and dreamy figures are easily dealt with and easily defeated, but well-connected and well-organized bodies under the leadership of a dynamic personality can pose a serious threat. The followers of Jesus—and his enemies—knew that all this planning and preparation in a messianic key portended something significant, probably a coming march on Jerusalem when the messianic Kingdom would be definitively proclaimed. What might happen then was anyone's guess, but it would certainly mean something dramatic.

An interesting episode involving two of the Twelve Apostles, James and John, throws additional light on the atmosphere among the company surrounding Jesus. As they saw the careful preparations, the training of disciples, Jesus' growing reputation, his sure grasp of his own strategy, and the heightened anticipation of coming events, these two "sons of thunder" approached their sovereign-in-exile with a special request: "When you come into your kingdom, grant that we may sit at your right hand and at your left" (cf. Mark 10:37). In other words: "We see you are about to make your decisive move. We would like to be Prime Minister and Secretary of State in the powerful kingdom you are about to establish." When the other Apostles heard of the request, they were indignant at the two brothers for stealing a march on them— some of them were apparently harboring similar ambitions—and it became the occasion for a salutary teaching from Jesus about authority.

Those who wished to be great—a desire Jesus wanted his disciples to possess—needed to understand what true greatness really meant. It was not in being "top dog" but in taking the lowest place and in serving the rest, just as he, the Master and King, was serving those he was leading.

The episode also showed how inadequate the disciples' understanding was of the kind of Kingdom Jesus planned to establish. To help prepare them for what was coming, Jesus began to warn them of the necessary path he was going to follow if his demonic and human enemies were to be conquered and his reign brought about. He spoke of being taken prisoner and being put to death. He alluded mysteriously to rising from the dead. None of this made sense to his disciples. Despite having heard his teaching, they had not yet grasped the fundamentally spiritual nature of his Kingdom. And the idea that the Messiah would not immediately conquer his enemies but would seemingly be conquered by them ran counter to all their expectations. At one point, in order to steel them for coming events, Jesus took the leaders among them, Peter, James, and John, up a mountain, and there he allowed them to encounter something of his real identity. He was seen by them in conversation with Moses and Elijah, revealing himself as the fulfillment of the Law and the Prophets, and about to inaugurate a new Exodus. The disciples were given a glimpse of his divinity shining through his humanity, and they were overwhelmed and dazzled by the glory of it.

Finally, the anticipated event was announced to the company: Jesus was to march on Jerusalem. Thomas, the most hard-headedly realistic among the disciples, saw something of the likely consequences. "Let us go, and die with him," was his expression of loyalty (cf. John 11:13–16.) The Passover feast was coming, and tens of thousands of pilgrims were streaming into the holy city. The Romans, always fearing unrest at these pilgrim feasts when the city was filled to overflowing with zealous men, had stationed an extra cohort of soldiers at their fortress adjoining the Jewish Temple. All eyes were on Jesus. Everywhere people were wondering: Is he really the Messiah? Will he come to the feast? If he does come, will he attempt to take the city and establish himself as king? The crowds were restless and wondering; the temple authorities were troubled and fearful; the Romans were watchful and wary; the disciples were filled with conflicting presentiments, knowing that they had arrived at the crisis point for their beloved Master and the success or failure of the movement upon which they had staked their lives.

Into this maelstrom of hope, anxiety, fear, calculations of power, and dreams of glory, among a seething and incendiary pilgrim crowd, Jesus came, riding into Jerusalem on a royal mount like a returning monarch, with some among the populace doing him homage, shouting his praise, and proclaiming him the son of David, the long-desired King now coming into his inheritance. The city was stirred to its depths. All wondered what the next few days might bring.

Chapter 26
Jesus Establishes His Reign

Jesus entered Jerusalem in triumph, marching up to the Temple followed by the crowds, and, it is not too much to say, he took possession of it. God, veiled in humanity, was coming to his own house, and Jesus proceeded to act as the one who had ultimate authority there. He drove out the pack of money-changers with a whip, overturning their tables and scattering their coins and their records, and declared that the Temple was God's dwelling and was not to be profaned. He then took up his place in the Temple precincts and began to teach the crowds. Shaken by his acts, the High Priests responsible for the Temple sent a delegation to him. They nervously asked him, "By what authority are you doing all of this?" (cf. Matt. 21:23). It was a polite wording of a sterner message that ran: "We, not you, are in charge of the Temple and all its activities. You have no business here and no right to do what you are doing. Leave peaceably lest stiffer action be taken." They would have immediately seized Jesus, but the crowds were too many for them and were hanging on his words. When Jesus saw that the High Priests had rejected his claim to authority just as they had rejected that of John the Baptist, he sent them away unanswered.

So, it went for the next many days leading up to the Passover feast itself. Jesus would arrive at the Temple early in the day and would teach the gathered throng, while the Romans watched, and the High Priests, along with their Pharisee allies, ground their teeth looking for some way to stop him, whether because they thought him a false teacher or because they feared an armed insurrection and the iron hand of

Rome. Anticipation was intense. Then an opportunity fell into the laps of the Jewish authorities from an unexpected source. A man of Jesus' inner circle, Judas Iscariot, approached the High Priests and offered them the information they needed to capture Jesus when he was away from the crowds. One of Jesus' own picked men, who had lived with him during his entire public mission, who had heard his words, seen his miraculous deeds, and shared his mission and his close friendship, betrayed the Son of God into the hands of his enemies for thirty silver coins.

Early in the evening before Passover, Jesus held a gathering of the Twelve, a kind of council of war before the final thrust. It was a solemn moment for them. They realized that the hour of their Master had come. They had marched with him into the capital, stood with him as he claimed possession of the Temple, heard his prophetic denunciations of the religious authorities in that sacred place, and witnessed the response of the populace. Now at the time of Passover, a fitting feast for enacting the new Exodus and raising the banner of the new Kingdom, Jesus had called them together to celebrate the traditional Passover meal commemorating the act by which God had freed the Israelites from slavery. One can only imagine the mingled excitement, awe, and sobriety experienced by the Twelve. These were the men who had been privileged out of all humanity to share the mission of the long-foretold Messiah King: his labors, his plans, his desires, his battles, the most intimate aspects of his life. Now the king was about to enter into his own. They sensed themselves to be at the very heart of the world's drama, on the eve of the most significant events of all time. They gathered around their Master on this great occasion, eager to know what he might say or do.

The gathering proved equal to its anticipated importance, though the disciples did not fully realize until later all of what was occurring. Jesus was following a script written by the Father and unknown to his followers. Later they would grasp its full significance, once he had walked the road laid before him and had taught them what it meant. For now, Jesus told them many things about the coming Kingdom and what it would demand of them. He astonished them in stooping to the position of a slave by washing their feet, underlining his earlier teaching about the proper stance for those who followed him and served his mission. Most momentously, he gave them notice of the new Covenant he was about to establish with Israel. Having sent his betrayer away, he took the bread and wine of the Passover celebration, showed them to the disciples, and announced that he himself was the fulfillment and the true meaning of both the Exodus and the Sinai covenant. "This is my body, offered in sacrifice; this is my blood, the blood of the new and eternal covenant poured out for forgiveness and salvation" (cf. Matt. 26:26–29). He was giving them a lens through which to understand coming events: he was showing them that he was in the process of fulfilling the whole of the Law, with its history, its sacrifices, and its promises. Yet they still had no idea what it would cost their King to come into his Kingdom.

Having finished the meal, Jesus led his disciples to the private garden of Gethsemane where they had arranged to spend the night. There he commenced his final hand-to-hand combat with his enemies, both demonic and human. There he prayed, and for a time his humanity was nearly overwhelmed by the ghastly horror of what was coming upon him. It was not the physical torture alone that was troubling him: other men had faced similar pain with fortitude and endurance. It was rather the spiritual agony he was about to encounter that so unnerved his human nature. What could it have meant to be humanity's scapegoat, to have the entire weight of human guilt pressed upon his shoulders? What would it mean for him to be delivered, seemingly defenseless, into the pitiless hands of that dark spirit who hated God and ruled the world? Yet the new Adam stayed the course and emptied himself in love to the last. The whole of his earthly mission had been a continuous act of obedience to his heavenly Father. Now, even as he faced the ghastly prospect of crucifixion, he embraced his Father's will for the sake of those he had come to save. "If all this could pass me by, O Father; but only let your will be done" (cf. Matt. 26:39).

The story of the passion and death of the Messiah-king is well known and often told. Here it will be enough to recall it in brief outline. As had been arranged by Judas, the soldiers of the High Priest came upon Jesus in the middle of the night, seized him, and hailed him before the High Priest and the Council. The disciples, confused and taken unawares, fled in fear. Peter and John later recovered their wits and followed at a distance. At the house of the High Priest, Jesus was tried in the middle of the night by the Jewish authorities and declared to be a blasphemer who deserved death. Unable by Roman law to implement the death sentence, the Council went early in the morning to the Roman governor, Pontius Pilate, with the demand that he put Jesus to death on their behalf. *"We have a law," they said to him, "and by that law he ought to die, because he has made himself the Son of God"* (John 19:7). Yet knowing that Pilate would not be moved by internal matters of Jewish religion alone, they also accused Jesus of claiming to be king in place of Caesar, thus playing upon Pilate's worry of a Jewish insurrection. Pilate questioned Jesus and was intrigued by the answers he received. *"Are you the King of the Jews?"* he asked (Luke 23:3). Jesus told him, "If my kingdom were of this world, my servants would be in the streets fighting. But as it is, my kingdom is not of this world" (cf. John 18:35–36). Not finding Jesus politically dangerous or guilty of any obvious crime, Pilate wanted to let him go. But when it became clear that the only expedient action was to accede to the wishes of the High Priest and the Council, Pilate took the easy way out: he had Jesus first scourged and then consigned to death by crucifixion.

The prescribed thirty-nine lashes came close to killing Jesus; men often died under that scourge. He was then tied to a plank of wood that would be used as a crossbar and was forced through the streets to a hill called "The Skull" where the crucifixion would take place. Crucifixion was among the most brutal forms of execution ever devised. It was meant to last a number of days, maximizing pain, inducing terrific thirst, causing muscular convulsions throughout the body, and eventually killing by slow asphyxiation, all the time exposing the naked accused man to the derisive eyes of those passing by. It was reserved by the Romans for the worst of criminals, especially those guilty of treason. Jesus was nailed to the cross and crucified between two such criminals with the ironically intended but accurate explanation of his "crime" attached to the cross: "The King of the Jews." Being close to death already, Jesus endured his torture on the cross for only about six hours. The High Priests and the other religious leaders who had been powerless against Jesus' prophetic denunciations and had plotted in vain to trap him now came to gloat over their victory. "You called yourself the Son of God and the King of Israel," they taunted him. "Fool! Let us see if you can come down from that cross!" (cf. Mark 15:30).

With Jesus at that final hour were only Mary his mother, faithful to the last and accompanied by a few other women followers, and his beloved disciple John. Peter, caught by fear, had denied any connection with him; he and Jesus' other friends and disciples were nowhere to be found. After finally entrusting the care of his mother to John, Jesus said the words "It is accomplished!" and with a great cry, he died (cf. John 19:30). Thus did the true King do valiant battle against his demonic foes, offer his life in sacrifice for a guilty humanity, and come into his reign.

Chapter 27
Resurrection: The Empty Tomb

From the point of view of his close followers, the capture and death of Jesus was a devastating and disorienting event. It seemed to make no sense and to throw all their hopes and beliefs into confusion. From the beginning, they had seen Jesus deal with his mission in masterful fashion. They had known him not only to be a decisive leader but a person of such spiritual authority that they had come to believe him a unique manifestation of God's power and presence on earth. Again and again, he had skillfully put his enemies to confusion. He had healed the sick, raised the dead, cast out demons with a word, and opened minds and hearts to the Father in ways that had never before been known. He had spoken constantly of his plans to establish the Kingdom of God. Nothing had been too much for him; no obstacle had slowed his advance. All the disciples' faith in God, all their future hopes for themselves and for their people, had come to be focused on their beloved Messiah and his mission. And now in the space of less than a day, that whole edifice had come crashing down around them and had crumbled into dust. The Master who had seemed on the cusp of a great victory had been taken in secret and eliminated by his enemies. The one they had thought to be the true King of Israel had been decisively and irrevocably defeated. The man they had dared to think was the very Son of God had been horribly and shamefully treated and was now dead. The messianic mission upon which they had staked their lives had failed. All was lost.

The demonic mind, equally in the dark, was reveling in a different set of thoughts. Satan had seen this new prophet arise, as he had seen many before, and he had been battling against him according to the resources allowed him. He had attacked him with seductions and temptations; he had tried to frighten him, to flatter him, and to discourage him; he had stirred up his servants against him. But he could gain no foothold. The man had not only dodged every dart and sidestepped every carefully laid trap, but he had shown a strange power of undoing Satan's rule. Yet worse, he had taught and empowered others to do the same. The whole matter had been perplexing and infuriating. Yet, the Devil knew that he held the final card. Whatever the man might say or do, in the end he was a son of Adam, a mortal under the curse of death, and sooner or later—sooner if it could be managed—he would die. He would then be gathered under Satan's dominion with all his miserable human fellows and share the fate of a fallen and rebel race. And now at last Satan had cleverly succeeded—so he thought—in putting into effect the plan that had caught Jesus and killed him. The victory would be so much the sweeter for having been so long deflected and delayed. He sped to embrace this soul newly detached from its physical remains and was more than usually eager to feast upon the latest of his conquests, to enjoy that special moment when he could reveal himself as overlord and could relish the horror of his human slave, the only glimmer of satisfaction left to his twisted spirit.

But the greed and gloating of the Devil turned rapidly into something very different. He did indeed meet the new arrival; he did encounter the soul of the man he had connived to have killed. But something strange, entirely new to his experience, began to happen. The "prisoner" did not come sad and defeated, bound in chains of darkness and surrounded by the triumphant laughter of demons. Instead, he came wrapped in a blinding, searing light, such as had never before blazed in that dark dungeon. He came forward upright and strong, with authority and power, sending the demons shrieking in dismay, and boldly advancing upon the Prince of Darkness. Now the mind of Satan was filled with fear and foreboding, as the true identity of this mysterious figure broke upon him, and he saw too late that the trap he had so cleverly laid for his enemy had sprung upon himself. The idea that the divine *Logos* might humbly unite himself to humanity had never entered the darkest corner of his proud mind. His cunning craftiness had been overthrown by God's seeming foolishness. By bringing a criminal's death upon the innocent Son of God, he had unwittingly opened death's door. Now the Lord of Life himself was demanding from him the keys of death, was announcing the Good News to all who had been chained by it, and was leading them out of the Devil's dungeon into freedom and light.

Meanwhile, in the visible world, the body of Jesus still lay in the cave-like tomb that had been provided by a sympathetic man of wealth. Pilate had ordered the tomb to be tightly shut, sealed, and guarded by a unit of soldiery: one never knew what these fanatical Jews might attempt once they had been inflamed with ideas of their Messiah. The company of Jesus' disciples were dispirited and frightened, fearing for their lives and facing a blank future. When on the third day after Jesus had been buried, on the first day of the new week, some women of the company went to the tomb to perform the customary preparations that they had been unable to complete because of the oncoming Sabbath, they were surprised to find the soldiers scattered, the stone that had sealed the tomb rolled away, and the tomb itself empty. All they found within it were the burial clothes. More wonderful still, they were given an angelic vision and were told that Jesus was not dead, but alive. Among the women was Mary of Magdala, one of those who had faithfully followed Jesus and had stood near him and his mother at the crucifixion. While she was wondering what might have happened to her beloved Master, he himself appeared to her, calling her by name.

"Go to my brethren," he told her, *"and say to them, I am ascending to my Father and your Father, to my God and your God"* (John 20:17). She ran off to tell the Apostles and the other disciples what had happened, that Jesus was alive, and that she had seen him and spoken with him. They too came, and running to the tomb they found it just as Mary and the other women had told them.

So it was that the Kingdom of Heaven gained an unshakable foothold on earth. The Messiah had completed his mission and had accomplished the salvation of his people, not merely freeing them from human oppression or physical disease but lifting the ancient curse, the source of all their misery. By the willing offering of himself, Jesus had paid the debt of sin. By rising from the dead, Jesus had conquered the demonic enemy and returned humanity to its original form, restoring it from corruption and undoing death. The Devil's rule was approaching its end.

During the next forty days, Jesus spent time with his disciples and friends, consoling them and preparing them for their coming mission. Yet his presence among them was different from what it had been before he went to his death. He was still a man, someone who could walk with them, speak to them, share a meal with them, be seen and heard and touched. Yet he was no longer confined to normal human limitations; his existence was on a different and higher level. He came and went mysteriously, unhindered by walls and doors, unshackled by time or space. He was undoubtedly the same person, and yet in some way he was transformed and therefore not easily recognized. His disciples were awed and dumbfounded by his presence, filled with a new joy and hope, but still not knowing what this resurrection might mean.

In the few weeks that he remained with them, Jesus enabled his followers to see what God had originally intended humanity to be, now renewed and freed from corruption. He was giving them a glimpse of their own future, of what they too would possess as his disciples. He was especially concerned to see that they who were to spearhead the coming mission as his witnesses understood that he had truly risen from the dead and was now beyond the reach of death, and that his plan to establish the Kingdom and to save humanity was not ended or defeated but had just begun.

Chapter 28
Ascension and Pentecost

At a certain point when Jesus was bodily present to his disciples after the Resurrection, they asked him a pertinent question: "Lord, will you now restore the Kingdom to Israel?" (cf. Acts 1:6). It seemed the obvious thing for him to do. The disciples had passed through a dark night of sorrow, as they had witnessed their mighty captain and beloved king seemingly destroyed by his enemies. But that night of sadness and defeat had turned into a morning of bright hope. The Messiah had risen from the dead and was now beyond death's grip. Their imaginations were stirred by the possibilities of coming victories. What a fitting revenge it would be, if Jesus should now walk calmly in among the High Priests and the Council of Elders, those who had conspired to put him to death and had taunted him while he was on the cross, and watch their shock and dismay. What a scene of triumph it would be if Jesus should return to the Temple and again gather the crowds, this time to see and hear their King risen from the dead. Nothing would stop them led by such a divinely powerful figure. All Israel would flock to their standard, all their foreign enemies would flee before them, and the messianic kingdom for which they had been longing would be finally and triumphantly established.

As usual, Jesus was thinking and acting on an entirely different and higher plane. Mere human comeuppance meant nothing to him; he was not interested in that kind of petty revenge. And there were other paramount considerations he had in view. The time would indeed come when the Kingdom would be fully established, when every eye would see him, when his coming would be like the lightning flashing across the sky. But there was a catch involved: on that day, when all would see Jesus unveiled as true Lord, all would be caught in whatever state of heart they possessed. That would be the day of final judgment from which there could be no reprieve. The Divine Word had not lowered himself to a human state and slipped into enemy-held territory in disguise only to judge and condemn a rebel populace; he could have accomplished that far more easily from his place in heaven. He had come among them to heal their rebellious hearts and to win back to his friendship any who were willing before the inevitable day of reckoning came. It would do fallen humans no good to see Christ in his glory while they remained in a state of inner corruption. Satan himself had seen God and knew him well enough; but the sight of that majestic light only tortured him and confirmed him in his envious rebellion.

Jesus now showed the disciples the manner by which his Kingdom would grow. During the time of his public mission, he had preached the Good News up and down Palestine mainly among the Jews. He had performed signs enough to convince the open-hearted of the presence of God, but not so powerfully as to compel those whose minds and hearts were closed. Hence his human "disguise." He had carefully arranged matters such that those who were seeking God, who felt deeply their exile from Eden and were looking for their lost Lord, would find him; and those who were not seeking, who had desired independence from their Maker and were content with the devil's rule, would not find him. His words, his signs, and the quality of his presence had laid open the inner hearts of all he met, and each had risen or fallen according to that inner stance.

During his time of mission, Jesus had gathered the company of disciples to himself, had taught them, and had bonded them together in close fraternity. Now he was making them witnesses of the greatest of his signs, his triumph over darkness and death. They were to continue his work and carry the news of the Kingdom to the world, making the same proclamation of forgiveness for sins, reproducing the same kinds of signs, bringing the same promise of peace with God and freedom from the Devil's rule, announcing his resurrection, and offering the gift of divine life. The same testing of hearts and minds that Jesus had begun would continue and be extended through the world and down the generations by his mysterious presence in the words and deeds of his followers. His earthly mission had been to the house of Israel; theirs was to be to the Gentiles. "Go and make disciples of all the nations," he told them, "baptizing them and teaching them; and I will be with you to the end" (cf. Matt. 28:19-20). Thus, the promise made to Abraham, that all the nations would be blessed by his descendants, would come to fulfillment.

Jesus arranged for one last meeting with the Apostles, leading them up a mountain and giving them his final instructions. He said to them, *All authority in heaven and on earth has been given to me*" (Matt. 28:18). He directed them to remain in Jerusalem and to wait for a new power to come upon them. He was then taken bodily from their sight. The Divine *Logos*, having united himself to humanity such that he might experience the plight of his mortal creatures even to death, was now bringing humanity into the heart of God such that they might experience the blessedness of the Trinity's life. He was completing the astounding exchange that had begun at the time of the Incarnation. He who had lowered himself and embraced the state of slaves was now lifted to the supreme place and was crowned in the presence of the heavenly Father as true King. God had then become man; and now man was becoming God. The disciples stood watching in amazement as Jesus was taken from them, and angelic messengers suddenly appeared to them. *"Men of Galilee,"* they said, *"why do you stand looking into heaven? This Jesus, who was taken up from you into heaven, will come in the same way as you saw him go into heaven"* (Acts 1:11).

The disciples, who just a few weeks earlier had been plagued by sorrow and fear, now began to understand certain things Jesus had told them before he had been crucified. He had said that he was leaving them but, strangely, that his going away would be better for them and for the world. He had spoken of sending his own Spirit, who would strengthen them and lead them into the fullness of truth. Now his meaning was getting clearer. By this means, Jesus would continue to be with them, less tangibly but more completely. No longer would he be only an outward presence necessarily constrained in his dealings with them by the limits of time, space, and sense. He would now come to them invisibly but more intimately, inhabiting their very minds and spirits one by one, imparting his own divine life to each disciple from within. They would thus be united to him—and through him to one another—in the deepest possible way. They would in a sense become him, not only imitating and obeying him but participating in his inner life. This would be the fulfillment of the promise of a new covenant, a pact and a law written on the hearts of a new humanity.

The disciples met together in Jerusalem and chose a successor for the one who had betrayed Jesus and who had since taken his own life. Their gathering took place at the time of another of the great pilgrim feasts, the Feast of Weeks, or Pentecost. On this feast, the Jews celebrated their wheat harvest, but of greater symbolic importance, they commemorated the giving of the law through Moses on Mt. Sinai. It was a fitting day for the fulfillment of that law to take place, as a new covenant was about to be sealed by the coming of the Holy Spirit. As they gathered together in prayer, accompanied by Jesus' mother, Mary, the Holy Spirit descended upon them and took up residence within them. As had happened when the first covenant was established, there were physical signs that marked God's presence. On this occasion it was not an earthquake and a trumpet blast but instead a mighty wind that made a great noise and amazed the inhabitants of Jerusalem.

Again there was fire, not as lightning flashing around the mountain but as flames resting on each of the disciples who were receiving the divine gift. Many Jews gathered to see what had caused the stir and were confronted by a group transformed by the Spirit's presence and power. Formerly tentative and unsure, the band of Jesus' followers now spoke with boldness and authority. Those who heard them experienced a miracle of comprehension: each heard the disciples speaking in his own tongue. The curse of Babel was unraveling, and humanity was being restored to its original unity. A new race was being born in the very midst of the old, and an explosion of divine life, largely hidden but of immense potency, was about to burst upon the world.

PART IV
THE LAST DAYS:
THE MESSIANIC AGE

Chapter 29
The Second Coming of Christ
and the Life of Eternity

A story, if it is to have meaning, needs a plot, a line of development. It needs to be heading somewhere such that its conclusions can give significance to what happens along the way. Otherwise it is only Macbeth's "tale told by an idiot, full of sound and fury, signifying nothing." God has shown us the broad outlines of humanity's often hidden drama, first through the history of the Chosen people, through the Mosaic Law and the Hebrew prophets, and then decisively by his revelation in Christ. He has told us where the story is headed and what will be required for its fulfillment. The Christian narrative thus addresses the future as well as the present and the past. Yet it is important, especially in our time of secularized religions that claim to be able to predict the future pattern of this-worldly events and to know "the right side of history," that we be clear about just what sort of information and hints we have been given. God has revealed the future to us to the degree that it will help us deal confidently with present duties. He has told us what we need to know, not everything our eager curiosity would like to know. He has not made the future so certain and tidy that we can rest in a false security and relax the need for faith, nor abandon the responsibility of free beings to make choices that will have lasting consequences.

Anyone who reads the words of Jesus attentively cannot fail to be impressed by how constantly he refers all present matters to a future reckoning. He entirely relativizes our current existence, insisting that the significance of what we now do can be known only in reference to its importance in the scale of eternal truths. Everything is to be judged by the light of that last day; all human acts and endeavors have meaning only insofar as they remain meaningful by the measure of eternity. This emphasis does not lessen the importance of our present life; if anything, it vastly increases that importance. But it robs the present of any particular significance in and of itself. According to the lens given by Jesus, the whole of our present life, all that we call the world and its activities, is to be seen, evaluated, and acted upon with eternity in view.

What then have we been told about the future? Where is the great drama leading?

First: we know that the current age, what we call the history of the world, will come to a decisive close and that its closing will not be the end but rather the beginning of the ultimate human story. We are still at the dawn of things, undergoing the birth-pangs of a coming Kingdom. When this age ends with the second coming of Christ, the preliminaries will be over, humanity will have come of age, and the real and lasting story will commence.

Second: we know that "eternity" does not simply mean "a very, very long time." It is difficult for creatures whose medium of existence is time to grasp the idea of time itself as part of creation. But God is not bound by time; he is not a very old being. His existence is an eternal present beyond time. When humans are granted the promise of eternal life, it does not mean that they will exist in some future state for billions of years according to our current conception of things. The idea carries a certain horror with it; life as we now experience it would be intolerable under such conditions, not only because of present suffering but because the essence of human life in this age is activity and progress toward a hoped-for goal. We are made to desire our full creation, and we yearn to be clothed in our final form. The promise of eternal life in an eternal Kingdom is the fulfillment of that yearning, in a state of being beyond our current experience, and in some mysterious way, beyond time itself.

Third: we know that all that we most hope for, our intimations of beauty and ecstasy, our search for loving communion, our desire for justice, our yearning for life, our fear and humiliation in the face of death, our longing to be "home," will have their true fulfillment. The renewed human race will dwell, body and soul, in a re-created world that will not simply destroy but will complete our current existence.

Fourth: we know that at the end of this preliminary age, this age of the testing of hearts, there will be a great judgment. At that event, all stories will be told truly, all that has lain in darkness will be brought to light, all lies will be exploded, all the works of the Devil will be destroyed, and every heart, the deepest essence of each person, will be laid bare in the light of the all-searching gaze of God. It will then become clear who has been made worthy of the heavenly life graciously offered by God in Christ. The consequences of human freedom will be gathered in, and each immortal being will live in communion with what each has chosen to imitate, love, and become, whether divine or demonic.

Lastly: we know that the life of the Kingdom, the breaking in of eternity upon time, has already begun. Its full expression remains a future event; but already we possess a foretaste, a downpayment of the life of eternity. Renewed humans, even while on earth, are in a sense living among the heavenly and timeless realities, not just symbolically but really. Christ's coming and his rising from the dead have launched humanity into a new age in which heaven's eternal life is percolating among us and invisible and timeless realities are laid open to us. Just as Jesus has ascended bodily to the heavenly state and yet is still present on earth, so Christians are living amid the strictures of fallen humanity and of time and space, and yet are present in heaven. The time will come when this "in-between" age, this age when the eternal Kingdom is "already but not yet" established, will be closed and the long-prepared wedding of God and humanity will be consummated.

We have thus been given the deep plot of our story, such that we can live in reasoned and joyful hope for what is coming. But lest we wander away from the true plot of humanity's drama, we should also be aware of what we have not been told.

While we know that this age will someday come to an end, we have no idea when that end might be. We have explicitly not been told the day or the hour. Next year? Fifty years from now? A hundred? Ten thousand? Because we know that the form of this world is passing away, we have been counseled to deal with it contingently and as not worthy of our deepest loves, an attitude necessary for all the ages of history. But beyond that we don't know.

While we know that God is at work in human history, that his providence ultimately and mysteriously rules human destinies, we have little knowledge as to how that providence works in detail. We are in no position to make judgments about why certain events go the way they do, or how God will make his presence felt in human affairs. Apart from a few exceptions that have to do with the fortunes of his Chosen People, God has kept these matters to himself. Additionally, we have not been told in any detail the course of God's Kingdom on earth in the Church, whether its influence will grow to overflowing with the passage of years, or wane to near disappearance, or fluctuate in different times and places. We know only that the Gospel will be presented to all. *"When the Son of man comes, will he find faith on earth?"* (Luke 18:8). Jesus purposely left his question unanswered.

While we know of a promised life of joy and fulfillment in the coming age, we know very little about the specific details of eternity, an ignorance that is hardly surprising given that we are dealing with a plane of existence beyond our current experience. And while we know that a judgment is coming, that this age and our brief lives here are a time of testing, we have not been given access to human hearts such that we can judge with certainty what the individual test results will be, neither for ourselves nor for others. We have been given clear directions about good and evil behavior, about what characterizes the Kingdom of Heaven and what bears the mark of rebellion and corruption, but we are unable to divide the human race into the simply good and the simply evil, into those who will ultimately inherit the Kingdom and those who will not, a judgment that only a just and all-knowing God can make.

The effect of this knowledge of the future, of what we know and what we do not know, keeps Christians both hopeful and humble in the midst of the complex and often puzzling course of their own lives, and in the face of the possibilities and tragedies of broader world events and developments. Christians know that they and the world are in the care of God, and that the story God has authored will come to its divinely ordained culmination. But they also know that God's providence does not overrule human freedom, and that much depends, for the ultimate destiny of themselves and others, on their choices and their actions. It thus comes about paradoxically that Christians, who though enmeshed in this world's life are not of this world, and whose hopes are lodged in a future beyond the confines of history, are in the best position to genuinely contribute to this world. Taught by Christ, they neither take the world's affairs too seriously on its own terms nor abandon them as valueless, and so are free to serve a passing world and its immortal inhabitants even as their hearts have been won by a coming Kingdom in which earth and heaven will be renewed. Meanwhile all their hope and longing center on the full arrival of that Kingdom, as they daily pray: *Maranatha*: "Come, Lord Jesus!"

Chapter 30
The Apostolic Age

The coming of the Holy Spirit inaugurated the apostolic age of the Church. Christ had said to Peter that the Church, the new humanity, would be built upon the rock of Peter's office, a foundational grace shared in some degree by the other Apostles. It was understood that the Apostles were not only appointed by Christ as the first leaders of his Church but that they were also given the responsibility and the divine gift of representing Jesus and his proclamation accurately and definitively to the world. The Church from that time on would claim to be "apostolic," founded on the witness, the teaching, and the office of the chosen companions of Jesus.

On the day of Pentecost when the Holy Spirit inhabited the disciples and made of them one organic living body, many Jews who heard the Apostles' proclamation of the Kingdom embraced the message and became disciples. From that time on, Peter and the Apostles began daily announcing the good news of the messianic Kingdom, filling Jerusalem with their teaching, working miraculous signs, and announcing the resurrection of Jesus as proof of his claim to divine kingship. Many joined their company, sharing their lives, their prayer, and their material goods, and forming the nucleus of a renewed human race. From its center in Jerusalem, the proclamation of the Kingdom began to spread throughout Palestine and into surrounding regions.

In keeping with the plan of God that the Jews were to be his instrument for the salvation of the world, the new messianic assembly—they were only given the name "Christians" sometime later—were an entirely Jewish body. The Apostles had no thought of starting a new religion; they remained believing Jews whose lives were deeply rooted in the history of their people. Because of this, they quickly ran into stiff opposition from some among their fellow Jews, especially those in positions of authority. The conflict between the Apostles and the Jewish authorities centered on the same questions that had caused those authorities to oppose Jesus. The first of these was the question as to whether or not Jesus really was the long-awaited Messiah. The Apostles said that he was; their opponents denied it. A second question had to do with the Apostles' claim that a new covenant had now been enjoined and that the Mosaic Law was being fulfilled in Christ. The Jewish leaders held that whatever change might take place with the arrival of the Messiah, he would certainly not change the Law. Jesus' readiness to adjust aspects of the Law such as rules about eating or keeping the Sabbath had shown him in their eyes to be a false messiah. Which brought things to the real point at issue. The Apostles claimed that Jesus was not only a prophet like Moses or a king like David, but that he was the divine Son of God, and that this remarkable fact was the authentic interpretation of the ancient messianic prophecies. If this were true, then Jesus certainly had the authority to say and do all that he did. If he really was the God of Israel himself mysteriously present among them, it was not surprising that he might initiate a new covenant and determine its conditions. But this was a claim that the majority of the Jewish authorities simply would not accept. So, they did their best to stamp out the new movement.

The attack on the disciples in Jerusalem forced many of them out of the city. In a result certainly not planned by their persecutors, by this means the Gospel of the Kingdom was further spread throughout Israel and among the Jews of the diaspora. Spearheading the fight against the followers of Jesus was an impressively energetic young man named Saul of Tarsus. Saul, or Paul according to the Greek rendering, was a devout and learned student of one of the most famous rabbis of his day. In his eagerness for the Law of his fathers, he chased down adherents of the new messianic movement wherever he could find them and threw them into jail, even outside of Israel. But in a remarkable turnaround, Paul himself became a disciple. He received a vision of the risen Christ, who laid upon him the office of Apostle. Much to the surprise of the young Christian community, their implacable fire-breathing opponent became their most energetic and effective apologist and evangelist.

Jesus had often taught his disciples that the pre-eminent sign of his presence among them, and the main witness to those who were not yet believers, would be their love for one another, their other-worldly unity amid a disunited race. Because of this, wherever the Apostles preached the Gospel they gathered those who became disciples into communities of faith, ordered assemblies, or churches. Each local church, living a pattern of charity, was united by the one Spirit they shared to the whole of new Israel, thus growing the universal Church around the world.

Something of the providential design of the Jewish diaspora could now be seen. There were communities of Jews living across the whole of the known world and connected by bonds of faith and kinship, in Egypt and all around the Mediterranean Sea, further east into Mesopotamia, and into the heart of Persia. Gathered around their synagogues were groups of Gentiles called "God-fearers," men and women who had been attracted by Israel's God and the moral order he taught but who had not embraced the whole of the Law, especially in its ceremonial aspects. The web of scattered Jewish communities was a kind of open road for the proclamation of the Gospel. To these communities the Apostles first went, speaking in synagogues and announcing the Gospel to Jews and God-fearers. Those who received the message, both Jews and Gentiles, became the foundation of the Christian churches from which the message continued to spread.

Our records are sketchy concerning the specific missionary work of most of the Apostles, but the traditions that have been handed on to us give some sense of the scope of their apostolic labors. From the original assembly in Jerusalem, they went in all directions, into Asia, Africa, and Europe. Peter was connected with Syria, Asia Minor, and Rome. Paul, about whose missionary work we know most, was active in Asia Minor, Greece, Rome, and possibly Spain. Both Peter and Paul were eventually martyred in Rome. Andrew went north to the Black Sea region, to what is now Armenia, Ukraine, and Bulgaria, as well as to Greece where he met his martyrdom. John was connected with Asia Minor, especially with the city of Ephesus; Philip with North Africa and Asia Minor; and Matthias with Armenia. Nathanael is thought to have brought the Gospel to parts of Arabia, Persia, and India; Thomas to Armenia and then India; Matthew to Persia; Simon and Jude to Egypt, Mesopotamia, and Persia. The two Jameses remained in Palestine, James the brother of John being early martyred, and James the kinsman of Jesus as head of the Jerusalem Church.

Before long there were growing communities of Christian believers in many lands, living and worshipping together under the Apostles' teaching and governance. In keeping with Jewish tradition, they were guided by the inspired Jewish Scriptures, understood now in the light of the Messiah's coming. As time went on, various of the Apostles or their disciples wrote down many of the words and deeds of Jesus for the sake of those who had not seen or known him, and some wrote letters to the growing churches. These apostolic writings allowed the "deposit" of faith to be passed on with clarity to new believers and future generations. As had been true for the Jewish Scriptures, these writings arose from the life of an already existing community under covenant with God, whose worship and organization the writings assumed. During the first hundred years or so of the Church's existence, a body of these writings came to be seen as a continuation of the Jewish Scriptures. They related the life and teaching, and especially the death and resurrection, of Jesus, Israel's promised Messiah, they announced the establishment of a new covenant, and they explained how the new covenant was a fulfillment of the Law and the Prophets.

When John, the son of Zebedee, the last surviving Apostle, died around the year 100, the apostolic age came to a close. The office of the Apostles in governance and in teaching was passed on, but the unique apostolic witness to the revelation of the Messiah had been completed. From this point on, the successors of the Apostles would carefully guard the apostolic "tradition," all that had been "handed on" by those graced foundation stones of the new humanity. A snapshot of the Christian church at the time of John's death would have shown something like ten or fifteen thousand believers from Spain to India, from Armenia to Ethiopia, putting down roots among many different peoples, united in doctrine and worship, and showing in germ the universal scope of the Church's mission. The Christians were still a very small group, hardly noticeable to the teeming populations among whom they lived and worked. But the leaven of the new human race was working according to God's favored method: small beginnings and organic developments that would eventually grow into strong currents of life. The race of humans had begun from one pair, Adam and Eve, and had grown through time by a pattern of slow growth, eventually to cover the earth with its millions. Now the new race of humans sprung from a new Adam and graced with a new Eve was following the same course. What began as a small trickle was to become through time a swelling stream, until finally it began to look like a mighty flood.

Chapter 31
The Church Through the Ages

The Incarnation did not end when Jesus slipped through the veil into the invisible world at his Ascension. In Jesus, God became man such that he could be seen, heard, and known. When the Spirit of Jesus came to dwell among his disciples at Pentecost, God once again took on human form, this time in the Church. Christians understood the Church to be Christ's body, not just in a metaphorical sense but as a mysterious reality. Just as the humanity of Jesus was the veiled road by which his divinity made itself known, so the humanity and materiality of the Church was the veiled road by which Jesus continued to make himself known through the Holy Spirit. The Church had thus both a human and a divine aspect, a shocking combination that has made it a constant source of delight, hope, and scandal to the world.

The word Christians have used to describe this union of the visible and invisible, the divine and the human, is *sacrament*. In the Christian vision, the visible world in its entirety possesses a sacramental dimension: it is the outward clothing of an invisible reality and a road to that hidden realm. This sacramentality is intensified in the Church, where Christ dwells visibly on earth. And in the seven sacraments of the Church the invisible presence of God is conveyed with unequaled potency and immediacy. For the Christian, the world is an enchanted place, hiding and partly revealing the invisible realities behind it. And the Church, for all its obvious humanity, is the outward clothing of Christ himself, as he continues his battle against Satan and ceaselessly offers forgiveness, reconciliation, and divine life to the human race until the time comes for the preliminaries to end.

To trace the 2,000-year history of the fortunes of Christ's body from the day of Pentecost would take us far beyond the constraints of this narrative. But it will be worth sketching very briefly the course of the colony of heaven as it has continued the mission of Christ down the years.

First, it will help to identify a challenge that arises in any attempt at giving an account of the Church's life. There is an inherent difficulty in grasping the dynamics of Church history, a problem that mirrors the difficulty of rightly seeing the progress of Jesus' public life. When Jesus is understood as both God and man, the extraordinary impression he made on all who met him has a clear explanation. If he really was God himself among us, waging a battle against spiritual forces and opening the hearts and minds of his hearers to a great promise and a momentous choice, then both the profound veneration and the furious opposition that he produced make sense. But this is a big "if." Those who deny the divinity of Christ need to go looking for other, more humanly explicable reasons for the adulation Jesus received and the opposition he provoked, and are then forced to create other Christs: the radical revolutionary, the erratic prophet, the demonic schemer, the misunderstood moralist, the gentle dreamer, none of which carry much conviction. The same holds true for Christ's body, the Church. If the Church is what it has always claimed to be—Christ really present on earth by the Holy Spirit—then both the ardent loyalty and the virulent hatred it has inspired through the ages make sense. But if it is a merely human organization, then other human factors have to be called in to explain its remarkable course through history. The high devotion it has so consistently engendered must be the result of masterful practices of deceit, and the hatred it has so often aroused must be due to its vicious crimes. Its stubborn existence and growth in the face of steady opposition and internal troubles can only point to hidden conspiracies and crafty manipulations of power. Otherwise how could the annoying thing keep going on as it does?

This difficulty of perception helps to explain the origin and longevity of the so-called "black legend" that has haunted the Church from its earliest days. Romans called the early Christians orgiastic cannibals and enemies of the human race. Since that time, there has been no lack of similar accusations: the Church has been labeled a pitiless persecutor, an oppressor of peoples, a hater of women, an opponent of science, an enemy of human liberty, an exterminator of Jews, a fomenter of war, and a haven of barbarism and ignorance. At the same time, the Church has been hailed as the ark of salvation, a friend to the poor and oppressed, a cradle of justice, a nurturer of scholarship and the arts, a wise teacher of the nations, a lover of freedom and opposer of tyrants, a benefactor of humanity, and the true home of everything truly human. In one view, the Church is a dark dictatorial figure, brutal and cunning, whose lies have often enslaved humanity, to which the only reasonable response is Voltaire's cry: "Annihilate the horrible thing!" In another view, the Church is a lovely and tender-hearted queenly figure, whose beauty and wisdom bring light and joy to an otherwise darkened and hopeless world, to which the proper response of the heart can only be: "Your dwelling is glorious, O City of God, our heavenly Mother!" (cf. Psa. 87:3). Darth Vadar or the Virgin Mary: the Church's perennial tendency to provoke such radically different responses is itself a sign of its divine nature and its connection to Christ.

A vision of heavenly worship was recorded by John the Apostle in which he saw people of every tribe, language, and nation, the regenerated human race, saved from death and delighting in divine life with God. The last two millennia have seen that prophetic vision significantly fulfilled. From its origins in Jerusalem, the Church has found its way, often by unpredictable and unlikely means, into every corner of the world. Inspired by the words and the Spirit of their Master, Christians have crossed seas, traversed deserts, and braved physical danger to bring the news of reconciliation with God to the peoples of the earth. The Church has also grown organically and has taken deep root in the cultural soil of whole nations and civilizations. Often persecuted during its first centuries, the Church penetrated the life of the Roman Empire, eventually becoming its preferred faith. Armenia was converted to the faith, Egypt and Ethiopia became centers of Christian life, and the Good News spread along the great eastern trade routes, arriving and establishing itself in Mesopotamia and Persia, in India, and even to the borders of China. Germanic and Slavic peoples of the north came under its influence. When the Mohammeden Empire arose and submerged much of the Asian and African church under its dominions, the previously backward peoples of northern Europe became the main bearers of Christian faith and put on strength and growth under the Church's influence. From that European center, the Gospel again spread rapidly in all directions. Soon there were large Christian communities living on the continents of the Americas, and seeds of Christian growth were sown in many parts of the world. As Europeans in their turn have increasingly turned their backs on their Christian heritage, the Gospel has flamed up anew in sub-Saharan Africa and parts of Asia. The ancient prophecies spoke of gentile kings who would bring their crowns and treasures to Jerusalem, seeking the God of Israel and submitting to his rule, and foretold a day when all the nations and even the distant coastlands would hear God's word and would be joined to the renewed Davidic Kingdom. Those prophecies have had a literal fulfillment, even if it is still a partial one, in the fortunes of the Christian Church through the centuries, as nations, peoples, and individuals across the globe have willingly embraced Christ as their King.

In every age, the human and imperfect element of the Church's life has been most visible: the persistent divisions among its adherents, the slow corruption of its divine life, its creeping forgetfulness of the invisible world, the all-too-human abuses of power or descent into avarice or sensuality among its leaders. Yet in every age, the Church mysteriously renews itself, gains adherents, and produces marvels of graced humanity as its invisible life regenerates its human matter and brings divine grace and strength to bear upon the world by means of weak and unworthy instruments. Jesus once said that he had come to cast fire upon the earth. The Church, his body, continues in every age to fuel the conflagration he began, setting hearts aflame amid battle, suffering, betrayal, and ultimate triumph.

Chapter 32
The Fight for the Human Race

When we cast our mind upon the world and try to take a broad view of what is going on around us, we naturally tend to see things under the limits of the present age and time. We look at various countries and peoples that populate the globe, and we situate them according to their current conditions. If we remember what is past, it is only as a way of shedding light on the present. The Roman Empire, once mighty, is now gone. So are the great Mesopotamian civilizations of the Assyrians and Babylonians. Ancient Egypt remains with us only in the artifacts it left behind. The Persian, Ptolemaic, and Seleucid Empires are known to specialists alone. All these have been relegated to the "dustbin of history." They once were, and now they are no more. By the logic of earthly time such a view of past civilizations and vanished peoples makes a certain sense. But when our gaze shifts to the Church, we can make the mistake of thinking about its existence and its fortunes in the same way. We can view the Church according to its current earthly presence and influence, and consider its health and its possible future in that light alone. We can look at past ages of the Church as vanished and gone, no longer in existence. Such a view might be accurate if the Church were like other human institutions. But the Church is not like other human institutions; it is a divine body, rooted in eternity, whose life is regulated by a rhythm that is not restricted by time or place.

If we could see the Church as it really is, if our view could be opened upon what the angels see, we would be presented with a very different picture. We would see a vast company beyond the reach of death, pulsating with divine brightness, basking in the beauty and light of God, powerful in spiritual weaponry, centered on the figure of their divine and beloved King, drenched in joy and eager for the continued gathering-in of the renewed human race. We would see an ever-growing body, as each generation on earth passed through the veil, from the land of shadows to the real world, and those who had been found faithful to their rightful king shook off the last traces of their mortality and were welcomed home. We would see the angels there, mighty spirits in the praise of God and in their help for humans. We would see the Twelve Apostles, still administering the Church's life, taking thought for their brothers and sisters who were fighting for their place in the Kingdom. We would see Mary, the Queen Mother, now revealed in all her beauty and authority, eager to bring aid with tender pity to those of her children still languishing under the ancient curse. We would see all the great ones from every age united together in friendship and joy, as each generation brought another rich harvest to the growing body of perfected humanity until the times were fulfilled and all were gathered in.

As we looked more intently, we would see that this glorious body was not in some distant place, in a galaxy far away, but was mysteriously inhabiting our own reality, though on a different and higher plane. We would see the thinness of the veil separating them from us, a veil through which there was constant communion and communication. We would see that all those who were now "alive" on earth, the whole of the world's population, were but a momentary snapshot of the actually existing human race. We would see the Christians living on earth as an outpost of the glorious company, sharing its divine life and potency. We would note that these earthly Christians were the least numerous and least potent members of the Church's body, inhabiting the outskirts of its life, still plagued by inner corruption and weakness, doing their best to carry the flag of the Kingdom for a brief time as they were put upon their trial.

One sometimes hears the question asked, whether or not the Church will survive. When the true nature of things is seen, the question becomes comical. Not only will the Church survive, if such an anemic word can describe the dynamism of its bursting life, but the Church is the only part of humanity that will survive. The Church is already beyond the ravages of time, free from the darkness of sin and the tyranny of the Devil, and its future is gloriously secure. The only question facing those still living on earth is whether they will they be joined to that bright race of divinized humans or insist on clinging to a dying and enslaved remnant of humanity that has no future but the shadows.

To lay out the deep history of humanity in this way is to address the genuine drama going on all around us. But it is a largely hidden drama. The perspective given us helps to explain great world events and significant historical developments, many of which remain an unsolvable riddle without it. But the drama itself usually proceeds under the surface of things, clothed in the stuff of normal daily life, working its way most profoundly in the minds and consciences, the hidden decisions and acts of each person, as they make their way among their families, their friends, and their fellow immortals along the path of life.

So, the battle for humanity will go on until the One who rules all destinies decides that the time of fulfillment has arrived. Christ continues in every age to build his Kingdom, to assault the powers of evil, to attack the fortress of darkness, and to set its captives free. Satan angrily attempts in every age to fend off that attack, trying to maintain his deceitful but now fragile sway over human souls, and to cling, however vainly, to his illegitimate power. Into that battle, into the complexities and mysteries of a graced creation, into a zone of light and shadow, of high hope and quiet despair, of beauty and corruption, sprung from a race of rebels, some allied to and enslaved by the Devil's tyranny and others struggling together against it by God's power, one fine day, each of us was born. Conceived from all eternity in the mind of God, created by him with a high purpose and a hoped-for destiny, we were brought into existence under the watchful and loving eye of the Lord of the Universe himself. In the high-stakes drama all around us, we have each been given a part to play, one that bears our name and no one else's. We each have the mercy of God to receive, a self to put to death, a Kingdom to gain, a battle to fight and spiritual enemies to slay, comrades to aid, rebels to win over, and a life of love to build, as we fulfill our task of inhabiting and reflecting the bright life and love of God refracted uniquely through each of his children. If the Father's hopes for us are fulfilled, we will embrace the part we have been given. We will receive the grace of forgiveness and new life, renounce the ways of God's enemy, walk the noble lowly road shown us by his Son, learn the lessons of humble warfare, and ultimately ascend the thrones prepared for us before the foundation of the world as kings and queens of God's creation. If we squander our high birthright, forget who we are, conform ourselves to the world's dark ways, and despise the promises held out to us, we will forfeit our place in the design of God and end as broken failures.

Here then is the real significance of that potent but often misused word: choice. The ancient battle rages all around us, and the adventure we were born for beckons. Life and death are held out to us and all heaven's bright company is aiding us. Our time on earth is short. Our eternal destiny awaits. The choice is in our hands.

References

Chesterton, G. K. *Heretics and Orthodoxy*. Reprint. Williams Bookseller, 2014.

Guardini, Romano. *The Lord*. Washington, DC: Regnery, 1982.

Lewis, C. S. *God in the Dock*. Grand Rapids, MI: Wm. B. Eerdmans, 2014.

Ratzinger, Joseph [Pope Benedict XVI]. *Jesus of Nazareth: From Baptism in the Jordan to the Transfiguration*. New York: Doubleday, 2007.

Rutledge, Fleming. *The Crucifixion: Understanding the Death of Jesus Christ*. Grand Rapids, MI: Wm. B. Eerdmans, 2015.

Tolkien, J. R. R. *Tolkien on Fairy-stories*. Ed. Verlyn Flieger. London: HarperCollins, 2014.

Biblical Sources

For those who wish to go deeper into the biblical sources for each chapter's content, see the following:

PART I

Chapter 1
Gen. 1:1
Ps. 33:6
Ws. 6:22–26
John 1:1–2
Col. 1:15–17
1 Tim. 1:17
1 Tim. 6:16

Chapter 2
Ps. 29:1–2
Ps. 103:20
Dan. 3:35–37
Ezek. 28:12ff.
Job 4:18
2 Pet. 2:4
Rev. 12:7–9

Chapter 3
Gen. 1–2
Ps. 8:3–4
Ps. 33:6–7,9
Ps. 104
Ps. 148:1–6
Isa. 45:18
Job 38:4–12
Rom. 1:20

Chapter 4
Gen. 2
Wis. 2:23

Chapter 5
Gen. 3

Chapter 6
Gen. 3

Chapter 7
Gen. 4:8
Gen. 6–8
Gen. 11

Chapter 8
Gen. 12
Deut. 7:6–8
Ps. 48:1–2
Ps. 87
Rom. 9:4–5
1 Cor. 10:1–4
Col. 2:16–17
Heb. 10:1

PART II

Chapter 9
Gen. 12–25
Ps. 110:4
Isa. 51:2
Sir. 44:19–21
Jth. 8:25–27
Matt. 22:32
John 8:33–58
Rom. 4
Gal. 3:6–7
Heb. 7:1–9
Heb. 11:8–13
Heb. 17–19
Gen. 14:17–20
Gen. 22

Chapter 10
Gen. 25:19–34
Gen. 28:11–15
Gen. 32:24–32
Gen. 39–40
Gen. 42
Exod. 1
Eccles. 44:19–23
Acts 7:2–18

Chapter 11
Exod. 1:8–17
Ps. 105
Exod. 2:2–10
Exod. 5–11

Chapter 12
Exod. 14
Exod. 19–20
Exod. 32
Exod. 25–26

Chapter 13
Num. 13–14
Num. 20
Num. 27:15–23
Ps. 78
Ps. 106

Chapter 14
1 Sam. 8–9
1 Sam. 16:1–13
1 Sam. 17
1 Sam. 18–20
1 Sam. 24
1 Sam. 26
1 Sam. 31
2 Sam. 1–5
2 Sam. 7:12–16
2 Sam. 7:18–29
2 Sam. 11–12
1 Chron. 28
Ps. 78:65–72
Ps. 89
Ps. 132
Sir. 49:13–20

Chapter 15
2 Chron. 1
2 Chron. 3–7
2 Kings 18:1–12
2 Kings 22:1–2
2 Kings 17
2 Kings 25

Chapter 16
Gen. 3:15
Deut. 18:15
Isa. 53
Dan. 2
1 Macc. 2

PART III

Chapter 17
Luke 1:29
Luke 1:34–35
Luke 1:46–55

Chapter 19
Matt. 2:19–23
Luke 3
John 1:19–34

Chapter 20
Luke 1:57–80
Luke 3:1–2
Matt. 3:1–12
John 1:19–28
Matt. 14:1–12
Matt. 3:13–17
Luke 3:21–22
Matt. 4:1–11
Luke 4:1–13

Chapter 21
Matt. 5–7

Chapter 22
Mark 2:40–45
Luke 5:12–16
Mark 5:21–24
Mark 5:35–43
Luke 7:11–17
John 11:38–44

Chapter 23
Matt. 14:13–21
Mark 6:30–44
Luke 9:10–17
Matt. 12:1–8
Mark 2:23–28
Luke 6:1–5

Chapter 25
Matt. 16:18–19
Matt. 17:1–13
Mark 9:2–8
John 12:6
John 13:29
John 12:20–26
Luke 10:11–12
Luke 9:10–17
Mark 10:35–45
Matt. 17:1–8
Mark 9:28
Matt. 21:1–11
Mark 11
Luke 19:28–48

Chapter 26
Matt. 26:14–16
Luke 22:1–6
Matt. 26:26–39
Mark 14:22–25
Luke 22:14–23
Matt. 26:36–46
Mark 14:32–43
Luke 22:39–46
Matt. 26:47–56
Matt. 27:33–43
John 19:26–30

Chapter 27
John 20:1–18
Luke 24:13–49
John 20:19–29
John 21:14

Chapter 28
Acts 2

PART IV

Chapter 30
Acts 1–11
Acts 13–28

Chapter 31
Rev. 7:9–12

Notes

Notes

Notes

Notes

Notes

Notes